HOW WE UNDERS

Learning t

ALAN MACFARLANE was born in Shillong, India, in 1941 and educated at the Dragon School, Sedbergh School, Oxford and London Universities. He is the author of over twenty published books, including *The Origins of English Individualism* (1978) and *Letters to Lily: On How the World Works* (2005). He has worked in England, Nepal, Japan and China as both an historian and anthropologist.

He was elected to the British Academy in 1986 and is now Emeritus Professor of Anthropology at the University of Cambridge and a Life Fellow of King's College, Cambridge.

Learning to
Be Modern
Jottings for James

ALAN MACFARLANE

2018

CAM RIVERS PUBLISHING

First published in Great Britain in 2018

5 Canterbury Close
Cambridge CB4 3QQ

www.cambridgerivers.com
press@cambridgerivers.com

Author: Alan Macfarlane
Series Editor: Zilan Wang
Editor: Sarah Harrison
Marketing Manager: James O'Sullivan
Typesetting and cover design: Jaimie Norman

The publication of this book has been supported by
the Kaifeng Foundation.

For James Wang, with my love

Alan Macfarlane, 2017

N. Adamson, D. Milner, P. Cartwright, S. Henderson, J. Broadhurst, P. Roberts, M. Evers.
J. Mermagen (on arm)   A. MacFarlane (on arm)
N. Bullock, J. Hunt, D. Milner-Moore (capt.), J. Travers, D. Walters, J. Whitty.

Contents

ONE

Becoming Modern

O NE OF MY strongest and most painful early memories is of an event that occurred on 18 October 1948, when I was six and three quarter years old. I woke to feel a lump at the end of my bed. When I unpacked the parcel I found it was a bus conductor's set – uniform, cap, ticket-punching machine. My delight was suddenly shattered when I remembered why it was there. My mother had told me the night before as she kissed me good-night that she would be gone when I woke the next morning. Although I couldn't really comprehend the full significance, she said she was going away to an Assamese Tea Estate (similar to the one we had come home from eighteen months before) more than five thousand miles away. I would get letters from her but not see her again for two years.

I did not cry and I played with my new toy, but remember emptiness. I went white when I heard my mother's voice on the phone from London before she caught her plane, as the following letter written on the same day by my grandmother with whom we lived:

My darling Iris – You must not be hurt when I tell you that neither of the children have shed a tear – it was a brilliant notion of yours to leave the presents and Alan has lived as a conductor ever since.

He turned white after hearing you on the telephone and again when your letter came this morning as we waited for the postman before he went to school. Fiona [my younger sister] is completely undisturbed and busy all day helping. They are being incredibly good and I hope there is a good supply of books as the Wonder Tales was read last night and "Arthur and His Knights" to-night… Lots and lots of love and don't fret, and be happy. Mummie.

It was to be the first and worst of recurrent partings which happened every two or three years another five times before my mother and father retired to England in 1966. Usually my mother went off at the end of summer. Picking blackberries, our last family outing together, still fills me with sadness.

My mother came home again at the end of my first term at the Dragon School when I was nearly nine and took me out for the day. She wrote to my father to describe what she found:

I arrived after lunch after an uneventful journey and was feeling pretty scared when I walked up to the front door of 6, Bardwell Road as you can imagine. Alan finally emerged from a room on my left and greeted me with a scared glance and a mumble that he had lost his shoe and disappeared into a pile of mackintoshes. I had been steeling myself for something of the sort and anyway hadn't time to burst into tears as matrons and housemasters wives appeared on all sides and had to be coped with. We got away in a few minutes

My heart sank rather at the completely silent little boy at my side – he has changed even more than Fiona and is no longer the "heart throb" of the family. Actually I didn't think he was looking very well, his face is much thinner and he has black lines under his eyes again and frowned a lot, however I hasten to add that he seems very happy at school and I expect after this first term (which is bound to be a strain) will probably have lost that anxious expression. It must have been an ordeal meeting me again and he told me later he didn't recognise me.

This world in a grain of sand, the deepest emotional shock of my life, has always interested me and now is the time to try to understand it and see whether it has a wider significance. In doing so, I shall try to show that many aspects of modernity and the world around us can be understood by examining my own experience.

* * *

One of the main themes of much of my life and intellectual efforts has been to understand the nature and origins of modernity. By 'modernity' I mean the separation of the different parts of our lives. In pre-modern societies, which include contemporary societies such as extreme Catholic, Muslim or Communist ones, the different spheres of life are 'embedded'. Religion and politics overlap, economy and society are not separated, and all these four fields overlap with others. This is very roughly how an anthropologist conceives of tribalism – all is connected, the world is 'enchanted' and relations with others are multi-stranded. In classic peasant societies there is some separation, but still the economy and society, politics and religion overlap. The fiction created in modern societies is that each institutional sphere is separate.

I say 'fiction', in fact we have never become totally 'modern' because these artificial separations are impossible to maintain.

So we have created hybrids which join such separated parts in different ways. Nevertheless, we clearly try to keep different parts of our lives apart – without letting things totally fall apart.

As I look back over my education and later experience I begin to see that I was being trained throughout my life to fit into such a divided 'modern' society, just as I see my own grandchildren being so trained today. It could be argued that in small-scale societies and in childhood things are largely undivided, that a child will not think of humans and things, of the natural and supernatural, the past and the present, the family and the economy, the world of the external 'reality' and the world of the inner imagination as firmly separated.

If this is so, one way to look at my story is to see it as a gradual extraction from a 'tribal', integrated world and my training to live in a rationally ordered and separated, world. The psychological and intellectual cost of doing this was what has long concerned me. The prison bars growing round the child and the sense of loss, alienation and the end of a certain form of enchantment which is present in Shakespeare, the metaphysical poets and Milton, Pope, Keats and Shelley, Tennyson and Yeats, reflect on this.

* * *

There are certain advantages and also dangers in using my own life and experience as a way of investigating English education. Among the advantages is that the experience is my own and deeply felt. Rather than having to rely on other studies, or other people's autobiographies, I can unite the different parts of a total experience that engraved itself on me and which I can examine from different angles. I can occasionally see the inner side of events and memories and piece together a continuous story over twenty-one years.

My experience was a typical example of a certain type of elite education of that period. Extreme in that I was educated in the top one or two percent of the British population at that time, the 1950's and early 1960's, who went for ten years to private boarding schools. These schools and universities were for this tiny minority, broadly representative. The Dragon School was more relaxed, innovative and liberal than many preparatory schools, but my public school, was a slightly old-fashioned and remote boarding school for the period, so the two experiences balanced each other. The small Oxford college to which I went was also very much in the middle in terms of teaching and culture for the period.

It is important to realize that the patterns of teaching organization in elite schools were reflected in day schools too, particularly grammar schools, even though the experience was more intense in the boarding environment.

I was one of the last generation of an old pattern of being sent home from the Empire. Being a late case, the features were made more dramatically visible, a kind of caricature, partly by the dramatic changes which would alter much of the outward structure very shortly afterwards, partly because in trying to mould us into an effective elite – the rulers – the process was much exaggerated, explicit, more thorough, more organized than in the majority of schools. So it is more easily dissected – the skeleton is on the surface of the animal rather than buried within.

So I was neither typical nor representative. And this fact is emphasized by my own particular character and family background. Others would not necessarily have had such an intelligent and empathetic mother. Others were not identical to me in my character, a mixture of doggedness, self-confidence, anxiety, and a desire to hold onto my childhood certainties.

* * *

If this account has any value, it is because my own experience, while unique, is part of a much wider pattern. Although the content and methods of English education have changed hugely over the last thousand years, the deep structure or shape has remained largely unchanged. This shape has several features.

One is that children were sent away from their homes at an early age to be 'educated' or trained. It has always been felt that the best people to train the young are strangers, non-kin.

As far back as the records go, that is to Anglo-Saxon England about 1500 years ago, we find the custom that young people should sever their link with their parents and never return, except for holidays.

A classic account of this pattern is by the Venetian Ambassador Trevisano in 1497. He wrote that 'the want of affection in the English is strongly manifested towards their children; for after having kept them at home till they arrive at the age of seven or nine years at the utmost, they put them out, both males and females, to hard service in the houses of other people, binding them generally for another seven to nine years. And these are called apprentices...' He felt that if the parents had taken their chil-dren back when their apprenticeship was over 'they might, perhaps, be excused' but noted that 'they never return'. Instead, they have to make their own way in the world, 'assisted by their patrons, not by their fathers, they also open a house and strive diligently by this means to make some fortune by themselves.' [1]

What one was sent away to depends on the relative wealth and status of the family. The poor sent their children off to be servants in other people's houses and farms, where they would not learn a craft skill, but would relieve their birth family of the cost of upbringing. Servanthood is one of the great, unusual, and distinctive features of English society. It was widespread from the medieval period onwards and often involved very young people being sent off to distant homes. It is an institution which was not even found on the Continent, let alone in the peasant civilizations of Asia (with the exception of Japan). Many in the 'working class', though this is an anachronistic term, that is perhaps the bottom third of the population, sent their children off as servants.

The young children would work as either household or farm servants and labourers and if they could save a little, might marry and then send off their children in turn. This phenomenon was transformed in the first half of the nineteenth century with industrialization and urbanization. The pattern remained in certain ways, that is the practice of sending poor children to work for others at eight or nine. Yet instead of becoming household or farm servants, they were sent to the mills and the mines.

At the next level up the social hierarchy, that is what one might call the lower and middle-middle classes, where the parents were a little independent and had some skills, there was a different pattern. These were the small producers, craftsmen, the smaller

---

1   *Italian Relation*, 24-6

merchants and shopkeepers, the husbandmen and yeomen farmers. They had some capital and a business of some sort and they would send their children off to learn a trade or craft by being apprenticed to a skilled 'master'. Here the work for the master was meant to be combined with the transmission of the 'arts and mystery' of his profession. As with servants, this could apply to girls as well as boys, though I suspect that it was mainly for boys.

Thus, at the same age, that is between about six and ten, a child would go off to live with his or her master and learn a craft – shoe-making, blacksmithing, being a shopkeeper, working in some small enterprise. The child would work more or less for free (just getting accommodation, food, minimal clothing and perhaps a small gift of pocket money), but in return they had an expectation that at the end of contract – and this was indeed a formal contract, the young person would be qualified and could set themselves up in that trade, perhaps with some help from his master and parents. If the child went off, say, at eight, the apprenticeship might last for seven years or more.

Among the skills to be transmitted was some basic literacy and numeracy, partly taught in the household but also in elementary schools or in the evenings, which would be necessary for most small business and craft activities. Even a blacksmith had to keep accounts and write to people.

This widespread system of apprenticeship is again unusual and English. In most agrarian civilizations the child would stay in the home and learn their father's occupation by imitation and co-working. This I have seen with blacksmiths, tailors and farmers in Nepal and would have been the case for most of history in China, India and elsewhere.

The above was the pattern for the ninety or more percent of the population in England below the level of the professional upper middle classes, from the Anglo-Saxon period through to the industrial revolution. The pattern for the other ten or so percent was different.

The first prototypes of the English public schools emerged next to churches, Westminster was reputedly founded in 594 AD and Canterbury about ten years later. So it is clear that institutionally the boarding school is very old, some would argue the oldest continuous institution in English history. Many of the famous foundations date from the fifteenth century, and there was a burst of the founding of free grammar schools in the sixteenth, as with my boarding school Sedbergh. These were schools for the gentry, richer yeomanry and larger merchants. The Universities of Oxford and Cambridge, dating from the end of the twelfth century, were fed by such schools.

These schools and the old universities were set up to teach skills, useful for people who would later go into one of the non-manual professional groups – the church, law, education, civil service, upper ranks of the army and navy, upper levels of trade and commerce, the running of landed estates, and, from the eighteenth century, imperial administration.

The skills were partly social, the ability to speak and distinguish accents, cultural knowledge (including dead languages and authors), etiquette, taste and discrimination. Those who went through such education were separated from the less 'polished' mass of the population and the universities put a final burnish on them.

Yet there was also an intellectual component, a training of memory, logic, rhetoric, mathematics, linguistics, which could be useful as generic skills for any cultivated professional group. These schools were mainly for boys, but there were clearly numerous equivalents for girls from the eighteenth century.

These elite institutions, which had been as widespread in relation to the size of the population in the fifteenth century as they were in the eighteenth, grew again rapidly along with population and the increasing size of the upper middle class during the nineteenth century. In the middle of the century, the schools and universities were reformed and made into explicit machines to train those who would run the expanding British Empire.

At the top were the two old universities of Oxford and Cambridge, as well as the late medieval universities of Scotland. The less than ten per cent who had gone through the grammar school/ public school stream would now taper down to one or two percent attending university.

* * *

Such was the general shape of the English educational system in the long centuries from the Anglo-Saxon to the middle of the nineteenth century. Two or three outstanding and unusual features of this system are worth noting.

Perhaps the most important is the way in which by taking education or training, or just growing up, out of the hands of the family, the world was changed. That all important separation between family and society, individual and society, society and economy, was built into the system.

This was the root of the autonomous and free individual, of the capitalist 'free' market, and of those deep separations of religion, politics, society and economy which constitutes modernity. This splitting of the atom of the family is painful and nearly impossible to achieve. It is an explosion or fission that has changed the world.

Secondly the fact that children learnt their culture from strangers meant that English schools, both in their formal structure and informal pressures, replaced the home as the locus of ethics and attitudes. Almost universally elsewhere, 'education' was to prepare the brain, or perhaps give some formal instruction in morals. But it was in the home that most of the moral and emotional education of children took place. In England, almost all 'education' took place after the age of eight in schools and amongst friends. Friends and teachers replaced the birth family. The education of body, mind, spirit and imagination was done outside the home. The home was for rest or 'holidays'.

By placing the education of all those above the level of wage labourers (servants) in the hands of formally and contractually appointed 'teachers', whether the master in an apprenticeship, or the master at school, or the Master of Arts at the University, it made it more likely that a more critical and objective teaching could take place.

The master of apprentices was skilled and had an incentive to improve his trade and be proud of his apprentices. The master at schools and university shared in the success of their pupils. They were themselves trained a little in methods of education, literate, open to newer ideas which they could pass on. This contrasts with the strong tendency towards conservatism, the fear of the dangers of experimentation, and the mix of power, authority and discipline in home-based education.

Finally, a strong feature of the education at the top level

of public, grammar and university education, was that it was
generic. In a society where there were so many career ladders
(army, navy, law, medicine, teaching, trade, manufacture, clergy,
administration, running estates) children very often did not
follow their parents' career schools and universities could not
specialize.

TWO

Indian infancy: India 1941-1947

T AKING 'FAMILY' TO mean both my father and my mother's ancestors, my family had been in Jamaica since the seventeenth century, India from the eighteenth, in China, Burma and Australia from the nineteenth. England was our 'home', but the wide British Empire was where we mainly drew our sustenance. It was a middle class family, professional and business people, lawyers, clergymen, army and navy, the occasional planter and academic.

Let me jump to the 1930's when my mother's parents were coming to the end of their life in India. My grandfather, William Rhodes James, was born in 1886 at Coonor in the Nilgiri Hills, India, the son of a coffee planter. Sent home to boarding school from 1895 - 1903 young, he went to Sandhurst and became a professional soldier, receiving a Military Cross in the First World War. He ended his military life as a Colonel in the 89th Punjab Regiment. Here he is with northern command in 1936 (second row, far right), and with his first privately owned car.

My grandmother was born in Mandalay, Burma, in 1896, the daughter of the first British lawyer in Upper Burma. She was taken and left in England at the age of eight. She was a talented artist and attended the Royal Academy Schools until it was closed in 196 due to the war. She then went back to Burma. She met my grandfather and they married in Maymyo in 1918. She would become the central figure in my upbringing.

My grandparents were constantly moving from house to house, my grandmother mostly packing up and transporting large sets of luggage, including many of the letters and photographs used in this book, as she moved from place to place

My father was born in El Paso, Texas in 1916, the son of a mining engineer. He was sent home aged twelve to Dollar Academy, a Scottish boarding school, and later trained as an engineer. He went out to India in 1936 to work on a tea plantation in Assam. He was an excellent games player. Here he

is (far right) in the Nazira Tea Company polo team in 1939.

My mother was born in Quetta, now Pakistan, in 1922. She was sent home at the age of six to be educated at six separate English schools. She was highly intelligent and hoped to go to university, but war was looming and she and her mother (with dogs) left for India in April 1939.

When war began in 1939 my father joined up and later helped to recruit the second Assam Regiment, where he served as a major. This photograph was taken toward the end of the war when the regiment had returned to Assam. My father is in the middle.

On one of my father's leaves he met my eighteen year old mother in Naini Tal and they married in Bareilly, India, in March 1941.

I was born on 20 December 1941 at the Welsh Mission hospital in Shillong. For three months my parents were together before my father was posted to a distant part of India. He only returned a few times during the next four years.

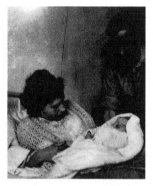

The family were apart for most of the time, but all except my father met at Agra at Christmas 1942 just after my first birthday. The picture includes from the left my grandfather, my mother's second brother Richard, soon to fight as a Chindit in Burma, her youngest brother Robert, later to be my main companion in England, my grandmother, my mother's oldest brother Billy, also soon to see fighting in Burma and finally my mother and myself.

My grandmother already shared my upbringing as my mother lived with her for the period when my father was away, so I was also with my youngest uncle Robert, half in this picture, who was only seven years older. I was fortunate that my early household, my grandparents and uncle Robert were already back in England when we returned in 1947. They formed a continuing presence when my parents were in India in later years. My father is here on one of his rare visits.

Despite my mother's constant worries about me, and three serious (one of them life-threatening) attacks of dysentery I seem to have grown reasonably and been a normal, quite cheerful, baby.

I was brought up by nannies ('ayahs') and learnt from very early on that I was one of the 'sahibs' who would one day ride, shoot, swim, play cricket and garden!

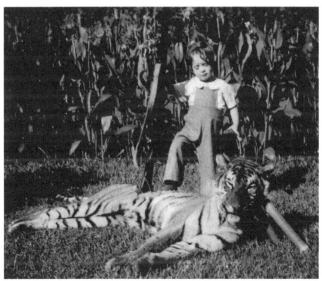

My mother was an adoring and compulsive carer, highly intelligent and creative and devoting all her love and attention on her children. I was joined by my first sister, Fiona, born in 1944, and she and I spent much of our childhood together.

My relations with my father were very close, even though he was often away.

My one really close friend in the Indian years seems to have been the sweeper's son. I learnt Urdu and spent a great deal of time with him.

At the end of the war my father returned to his job as a manager of a tea estate in the Assam valley, where my sister and I moved with my mother.

We were joined by my younger sister, Anne, born in June 1946.

I remember very little of these first five years, though clearly they were highly formative. The one event I think I remember was breaking my arm. It was not recognized as broken, so had to be re-broken by the doctor (without anaesthetic), a shock which I still recall.

My father was given his first leave and we left Assam for England in March 1947. Although my parents had constantly said they would never leave their children in English schools and be separated from them, they found themselves forced to start to do just this. There were no reasonable schools for English children in Assam. Furthermore, if I was to learn to be properly English, and to start 'climbing the ladder' towards a reasonable career, I must be 'sent back' in the way that had happened to generation after generation of my ancestors.

So ended the first chapter of my life, largely unremembered but perhaps more important than any other. I was adored and allowed great freedom. My mother was often lonely and I was occasionally seriously ill. But in later years I would look back on the warmth of those few years of an imperial childhood and want to return to see what that dimly remembered world was like. I visited Assam again on holidays from school when I was eleven and sixteen, but only returned properly to the area as an anthropologist to do fieldwork in the Himalayas in 1968. In the intervening years I would go through the indoctrination into English middle class culture which would fit me for my life ahead.

THREE

Dorset Days: 1947 – 1954

M Y FAMILY RETURNED in April 1947 to a cold and run-down England. We first assembled in north Oxford in a rented house. The first photograph includes almost all the important people in my subsequent family life. On the left is Robert, below him my grandfather and myself. Then at the back my father and mother (with Anne) and my grandmother and Fiona at the front. Then my two uncles Billy and Richard, back from the war, and below my grandmother's mother, Annie, back from Burma.

My other significant relatives were my father's parents. They appear on the bottom left (grandmother Florence) and middle back (grandfather Archie) in the second photograph with my father, uncles Billy and Robert, my mother and great grand-mother Annie and the three of us.

After a few months in Oxford we moved in 1948 to a rented house near Broadstone in the county of Dorset on the south coast. It was in woods, with a large garden and a gorse-covered heath behind. It was a wonderful place to grow up in, full of animals, secret places and beauty. Here is how I remembered it five years after we left it, when I was seventeen. And the house, seen from the lawn, and looking down towards the fruit nets are below.

During the seven years in Dorset I grew from a small child
into a teenager. From very early on my passions revolved
about sports, which my uncle Robert taught me. Robert was
a highly imaginative boy, then at public school at Sedbergh
and later to become a distinguished historian and Member of
Parliament. He infused games with magic, setting up cup
finals and competitions.

Many of my games revolved around books and films of the times, particularly the outlaw Robin Hood and notable western sharp shooters.

Other outdoor activities which were important in these years were learning to ride a bike, learning to fish for trout (on holidays with my Scottish grand-parents), playing with rubber boats and visits to the seaside.

It is more difficult to recapture my hobbies and games with models and toys. I was keen on playing with various small representations, soldiers, and animals, largely inspired by my uncle Robert who was a great model fan. As I have rarely thrown anything away, these are some of the toys I played with and my collections of chocolate bar wrappers, coins and other ephemera.

The whole family would sometimes assemble and the following shows all of the important people of my life, now five years on from our arrival at Oxford in 1947. Robert top left is nearly finished at Sedbergh, Richard is a schoolmaster at Haileybury College, my father is unusually wearing a tie. My grandparents on the left are as I remember them and uncle Billy will soon be married. I am now a prep school boy and my sister Fiona is quite grown up.

I grew up and continued to experiment, as with below with my uncle Richard's first car, a luxury for our family who had previously travelled by bus and train and occasionally by taxi.

I had been at kindergarten for one and a half terms and my first report shows what I learnt and what they thought of me.

REPORT for *Christmas* Term

SUBJECT.	*TERM MARK.	EXAM. MARK. %	PLACE IN FORM	SUBJECT.	TERM MARK.	EXAM MARKS. %	PLACE IN FORM
ENGLISH.				**SCRIPTURE.**			
Grammar ...				Catechism.			
Literature ...				**ART.**	A	18/20	2
Composition ...				Model Drawing ...			
Dictation ...				Freehand ,, ...			
Recitation ...	A	20/20	1st	Memory ,, ...			
Reading ...	A	18/20	2nd	Colour ,, ...			
Writing ...	B	18/20	2	**MUSIC.**			
HISTORY.				Singing ...			
English ...				Sight-Reading ...			
European ...				Piano ...			
GEOGRAPHY.				**DOMESTIC SUBJECTS.**			
MATHEMATICS.	A	20/20	1	Needlework ...			
Arithmetic ...				Handwork ...			
Mental Arithmetic				Woodwork ...			
Tables ...	A	18/20	2nd	**GENERAL KNOWLEDGE.**			
SCIENCE.				**DRILL.**			
Biology ...				Dancing.			
LANGUAGES.							
French Grammar							
,, Translation							
,, Composition							
,, Oral ...							
German ...				Height ...	ft.		in.
Latin Grammar ...				Weight ...	st.		lb.
,, Translation				Chest ...	in. to		in.

*A = Good.
B = Fairly Good.
C = Fair to Weak.
D = Very Weak.

ending *Feb* 19th 1948

Name *Alan Macfarlan* Age......years......months.

Form *I*...... Number of Pupils in Form.............. Average Age..........

TERMINAL EXAMINATION.

Total Marks possible...............

Total Marks gained................... Position in Form *2nd*......

Marks gained %......

Marks gained % by Head Pupil.............

ATTENDANCE.

Possible *62* half days. Absent......half days. Late......times.

GENERAL REPORT.

Conduct *Excellent*...............

Homework *Alan has made good progress*

General Remarks *in the term and a half he has*

been with us. He is a favourite with the other

children. We are very sorry he is going and feel

(Signed) *Winifred Whittington* *sure he will do well*

CLASS MISTRESS. *where ever he is.*

GAMES MISTRESS.

DANCING MISTRESS.

S. Whittington

HEAD MISTRESS.

Report considered by.......................

PARENT OR GUARDIAN.

Date.............................193......

Next Term begins............................

My formal education started at a primary school in nearby Broadstone, where I went in my new school uniform in the summer of 1948 aged six and a half. I had several friends from this time, with whom I am seen some months later, along with my sister.

The last report from my time there shows what I was learning and the schools views on my character. It does not show any great ability. I was above average in age and clearly not con-sidered to have much academic potential.

Some of my progress in writing in these years before I went off to boarding school can be seen in my first preserved letter, at the age of five and three quarters to my father and aged eight, a request to father Christmas at the age of nearly eight, and from a Scottish holiday when aged eight and a half, describing the catching of the trout seen in the photograph. This was written just before I went off to boarding school. I was encouraged to write as frequently as possible to my parents in India, and received long weekly letters, and occasional short stories, from my mother.

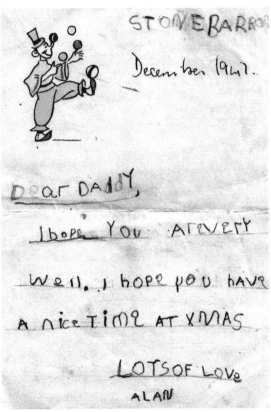

STONEBARRO

December 1947.

Dear DADDY,

I hope YOU Are Very

well. I hope you have

A nice Time at XMAS

LOTS OF Love

ALAN

Southlands school.
Broadstone,
Dorset.
Nov 25 th 1949:

Dear Father xmas,
you have.   I hope you are very well and
you have lots of Presnts for me. cave
I have a salinge ship. and a trin plees
and a meccano set and a woch and sum
sweets. and sum soldiers and farem anamals. with love.
      From
      Alan.

Corrydon   July 28 1950

Dear Mummy and Daddy and Ann,
we got the lovely Letter. We had
a nice Journey up from England.
I have cort a little trout and two
big ones. I am looking forward
to when all of you come back.
What fun we will have! I hope
we will go to Loch Morar fishing
we are writing because it is wet
and we can not go out to play.
we were going for a picnie but it
rained.   We had a picnic in the coach

FOUR

The Dragon School
Oxford: 1950-5

I N ORDER TO 'prepare' for the discipline and separations
of the private English boarding schools ('Public Schools'),
many were sent off to boarding 'preparatory schools', a unique
English institution for those aged between eight and thirteen.
I was fortunate to be sent to one of the best in the country,
the Dragon School in north Oxford, set up for the children of
Oxford and Cambridge academics. It was a school of about
four hundred boys and a few girls, run on liberal and advanced
lines by a family of excellent headmasters.

The school was founded by 'Skipper' Lynam in 1877. He
seems to have been an extraordinarily charismatic and liberal
schoolmaster who liked children and encouraged many different kinds of activities. The Dragon was soon turned into the
symbol of the school and can be seen here (overleaf) on the cover
of the school magazine, flying over the school bathing place at
the bottom and the towers of Oxford beyond.

The founder's family were still running the school when I went there. The Skipper's younger brother, 'Hum' was more or less retired but, Hum's son 'Joc' Lynam was the effective head. Here is Joc dressed for a performance of the operetta 'Trial by Jury'. He was also an extraoridinarily liberal, quirky and charming man who led the school with zest and humanity.

This gave the tone to a staff which included some of the best teachers in England. Here are four of the older ones, all of whom taught me. The one on the right, 'Bruno' was especially outstanding to my eyes since he was known to be a member of the Communist party, but also a brilliant producer of Shakespeare plays and Gilbert and Sullivan operas.

One of the most notable features of the school was that the staff were encourged to be the friends, almost the uncles, of the boys. Hence they were known (including the headmaster) by nicknames, usually invented by the boys themselves. We would address them as 'Spiv' or 'Guv' or 'Putty', as indicated in the following set of signatures with nicknames attached, signed in a boy's leaving book.

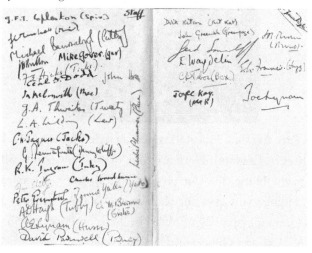

In fact the school was intentionally run as a kind of family, with the master's and their wives in the houses for the smaller boys known as 'Pa' and 'Ma'. And most of the staff clearly shared the early vision of the founding headmaster that boys were potentially intelligent, interesting and good younger friends. Consequently there was little bullying and a good deal of toleration and even encouragement for eccentricity and innovation. We were encouraged to grow in whatever shape we wished within reason and almost all of us were discovered to have some talent or other which we could be proud of, from mathematics to marbles, from classics to chess, from history to hop-scotch.

The fact that the school could draw on the resources of Oxford University for young teachers or cultural experiences, was one of the things that made it special. Another was its physical grounds and location. For the Skipper had sensibly placed the school just on the edge of the city and been able to buy a large area which ran down to the river Cherwell. It is this world, so much bigger to a child, that I remember best, and it is remembered fifty years later by my fellow Dragon and co-author of a book on the school, Jamie Bruce Lockhart, in the following diagram which outlines most of the important places in the central part of the school premises.

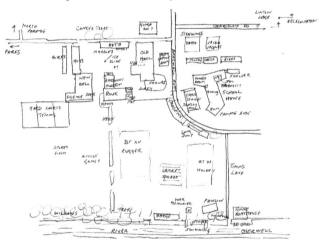

The focal point of the school was the 'Old Hall'. Here it was that we met every morning for prayers, where we did our indoor physical exercises, where we played many indoor games in the evenings and where the concerts at the end of term took place. Several of the classrooms in which I worked opened off this hall and I remember the atmosphere of cosy confusion.

The outside of the Old Hall from the south prominently featured the school lavatories (building with weather vane). The playground, where boys are doing physical exercises, was the main area for our own games, in particular for rolling marbles towards the fence running along the middle of the picture.

On the other side of the playground was the New Hall. It was here, on the ground floor, that I started my first lesson in Latin in 1950, and gradually progressed along the classes. The top floor held another performance and assembly area where the Shakespeare plays, Gilbert and Sullivan operas, speech days and other concerts were held. A mural at the end, since removed, urged us to be virtuous and strong.

Further classrooms were dotted around the playground, built to accommodate the growing number of pupils, numbering over four hundred when I was at the school. They were mostly boys, but there were always between about ten and twenty girls (a feature from the founding of the school when the Skipper had sent his daughters to the school). About two thirds were boarding, the rest were dayboys from Oxford, many of them children of academics. The 'huts' were just such classrooms and my final class, was in left-hand end of this building.

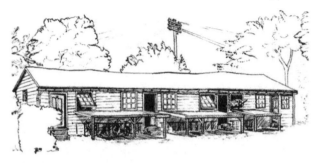

In the middle of the plaground was a building which housed a curious museum. Below the museum was the woodworking area where I constructucted my first wobbly toast-rack and first remember the smell of wood shavings and glue.

As well as the dozens of classrooms, an art room and science laboratory there were several rooms set aside for quiet reading, playing chess, and the meeting of the various school clubs. In some ways this was my first encounter with the 'Common Room' or 'Club Room' atmosphere which would continue through all my educational experiences.

Another special feature was the river. The atmosphere of the willow-surrounded Cherwell where we swam, fished, boated and just pottered about, is caught in this early water colour, which shows the changing rooms in the shape of a boat on the bank, and the diving board.

In order to be allowed to bathe on our own, we had to swim across the river and back in our clothes, the 'clothes test', which is being conducted below. Passing this test also gave us the privilege of using the school canoes and the punts which were kept in Timm's boatyard next to the school.

Probably the most important part of our lives was the playing of games. These were divided into formal games arranged by the school, such as rugger, football, hockey and cricket. It was on the ground below that I played my first game of rugger, becoming well-known as a plucky, if tiny, tackler of bigger boys. The fields for games stretched down to the river, as in the second picture, where the war memorial can be dimly seen – the nearest we had to a religious building in a school. (The boy in the foreground in both of the photographs is my friend Jamie Bruce Lockhart).

ALAN MACFARLANE

I was neither academically outstanding, nor very big and strong. But my days playing games with my uncle Robert in our Dorset home paid off and I became the only boy in my year who ended up with his first team colours for all four of the major games. Here I can be seen on the far right in the two most important teams, rugger and cricket. This gave great satisfaction to my family, and particularly my father.

CRICKET XI, 1955

J. Mermagen, G. Marsh, S. Poulter, J. Utin, W. Arber, A. Macfarlane
N. Raison, J. Travis, M. Evers (capt.), A. Miller, A. Denison-Smith

62

There were also many other kinds of competitive sports, including tennis, swimming competition and, as below, athletics. I was not particularly good at any of these, but enjoyed most of them. But what I enjoyed much more was ice skating. There were a number of very cold winters in the early 1950's and the headmaster loved skating (keeping a supply of 'Joc's skates' for boys who did not have them) and giving many extra holidays for us to skate on the great sheet of Port Meadow by the Thames, and setting up a skating rink on the lawn in front of the school house.

SCHOOL HOUSE RINK

Another type of activity organized by the school was drama. From the days of the Skipper the school had performed a Shakespeare play every year and so there were five such plays during my time. Although I never acted in them, we were encouraged to study the play and hugely enjoyed the performance, becoming soaked in the language and stories as part of our national heritage. Here is one of the five. Many of the boys (and a few girls) went on to meteoric careers, perhaps the most currently famous being Emma Watson, 'Hermione' in the Harry Potter films.

A MIDSUMMER NIGHT'S DREAM

R. McDougall, S. Crossman, R. Collins, M. Sharpe, R. Turner, D. Wilson, J. Gilman
H. Corll, S. Oliver, P. Hanley, J. Bird, J. Fletcher, P. Steadman
I. Moggridge, A. Denison-Smith, J. Travis, T. Hunt, F. Lambert, D. Sherwin White, A. Hunt, M. Evers, J. Chase, D. Parfit
Bridget Yates, Ann Woodhouse, J. Evers, T. Whears, Judith Owen, Caterham Simms-Smith, Janice Ure

My great delight in terms of performance, and something I remember better than almost anything else for its brilliant satire and glorious melodies, was the annual Gilbert and Sullivan performance. Again there were five in my time and I was in the second (Patience) and fifth (Iolanthe). I can be seen in the group photograph of Patience, fourth from the left in the front row, which shows how tiny I was. My rendering of a 'Love Sick Maiden' (bottom photo, extreme top left), left little to be desired. In Iolanthe (top right) I wore my coronet with distinction though appalled Bruno when I pretended to have gout and the parents complained at the appearance of a little boy with a serious limp.

'PATIENCE'

R. Hoare, A. Bennett, G. Harris, N. Cartwright, H. White, R. Houghton, J. Backus, R. Burleigh, M. Moore, I. Lindsay,
C. Woods, J. Plewes, A. Montgomery-Smith, A. Wynne, A. Rugg-Gunn, R. Saunders, N. Toone, T. Walsham, N. Berresford, A. Bere, R. Brooks,
M. Charles, A. Dunn, J. Ferguson, J. Acland, J. Davies, J. Marsh, F. Guinness, I. Burns, N. Owen, P. Bourke, J. Robson
Janet Thomson, A. Escritt, J. Gardner, A. Macfarlane, A. Phillips, A. Jackson, Susan Elliott, N. Ramsn, S. Macdonald, A. Denison-Smith,
M. Evers, I. Fletcher, D. Pakitt, I. Barrow, A. Brown, R. Lees.

There was a good spread of other music, including a school orchestra and, as below, a band set up by the boys with the help of a master. I was not a musician, but I enormously enjoyed learning to dance (mainly ballroom, Scottish and a little Latin American), sometimes to the accompaniment of 'The Mocking Birds'. I was also a member of a musical appreciation club where we listened to and discussed classical music. The teachers held little musical ensembles and played various humorous and tender pieces to us at end of term concerts.

When I arrived at the Dragon I spent two years in a small residential house, named after the housemaster. There I learnt to live with very little privacy, in close proximity to boys in the dormitories and showers and baths. It was all a shock. The food, illness, cold and hidden threats of possibly breaking rules made me anxious and wary, but also gave me the skills of participant-observation anthropology.

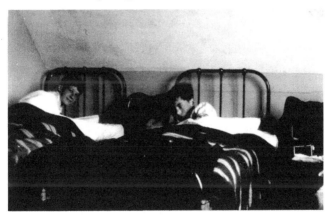

When we moved into the central School House, the conditions eased a good deal and the games and friendship and privacy increased. Particularly memorable were the evenings in winter when we sat round the fire and master's led sessions of folk songs from around the world.

The games we played in the winter with flashlights were particularly memorable, the lucky boys who had powerful ex-army flashlights like this were in a particularly favourable position in our pitched battles.

In order to survive and thrive, we learnt through the games, hobbies, sports and 'mucking about' how to make friends with strangers. The pool of friends was our dormitory, eating table, class, games team or just people we met about our own age and became close to.

I remember several of the boys at the end of my fourth year in my class Upper 4A, and my special friends are picked out in the 'Friends' list of the boy, now a retired Circuit Judge, who obtained these lists. We all had nicknames given us by other boys. Mine from my read-out initials (A.D.J. Macfarlane) and that of my second cousin J (onny) Mermagen from a likeness to his name.

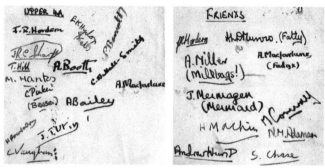

Groups of friends of this kind are well captured in the contemporary 'Just William' books, and we would spend our time playing elaborate games together, perhaps go out for a week-end with our friends' family, and otherwise show our affection in an innocent and open manner. Two of my closer friends, Jeremy Noakes and John Machin are shown in the photograph below with their school badges.

FORMAL TEACHING

I have left the matter of the formal, classroom, education to the end since it is both complicated and has to be set within the earlier context which, as we shall see, was just as important a part of our 'education' as what happened in class.

The organisation of the teaching and the wide range of teachers is shown from the list (with initials) of the teachers for the various core subjects. The school was divided into Lower, Middle and Upper, based on Classics (Latin) so over the five year period a boy would spend one or two years in each. I started in Lower V with Miss Owen, and ended up in Upper IIB, the third from top form. English, Mathematics and French was divided into sets, so it was possible to be in a high set and lower form, and vice versa. Thus, while I ended up in the third from top form, I was finally top in the second mathematics set. The other major subjects, divinity, geography, art, science, music, handicraft, carpentry and physical training were all important.

CLASSICS

Upper I. L. A. Wilding
,, IIA. J. H. R. Lynam and R. I. Kitson
,, IIB. H. E. P. Woodcock
,, IIIA. R. St. J. Yates
,, IIIB. J. B. Brown
,, IVA. F. R. Wylie
,, IVB. C. L. Tabor
,, V. F. E. Hicks
,, VI. A. D. Haigh
,, VII. C. H. Jaques
Middle I. W. A. C. Wilkinson
,, II. M. W. A. Gover
,, III. J. D. Britton
,, IV. J. O. Ure
,, V. J. M. Barrowclough
,, VI. C. P. Woodhouse
,, VII. L. C. Plummer
Lower I. G. S. Braddy
,, II. J. A. L. Chitty
,, III. G. Denison-Smith
,, IV. J. H. J. Greenish
,, V. Mrs. A. T. Owen
,, VI. Miss M. H. Bailey

ENGLISH

A1A J.B.B.
A1B C.H.J.
A3 G.S.B.
A4 L.A.W.
A5U H.E.P.W.
A5L M. J. Cooke, 189 Banbury Road, Oxford
B1 C.H.J.
B2 J.B.B.
B3 J.D.B.
B4 G. A. Barratt, Milford, Craven Arms, Shropshire
B5 M.W.A.G.
C1 M.W.A.G.
C2 G.S.B.
C3 Mrs. C. J. Bentlif, 104 Banbury Road, Oxford
C4 G.A.B.
C5 M.J.C.
D1 C.J.B.
D2 R.I.K.
D3 J.D.B.
D4 J.M.B.
D5 M.J.C.
E1 G. Stephenson
E2 A.T.O.
E3 M.H.B.

MATHEMATICS

A1 W.A.C.W., and G. C. Meister, 23 Sandfield Road, Headington
A2 J.A.L.C.
A3 F.E.H.
A4 A.D.H.
A5U L.C.P.
A5L H.E.P.W.
B1 W.A.C.W.
B2 C.P.W.
B3 L.C.P.
B4 J.H.J.G.
B5 F.E.H.
C1 W.A.C.W.
C2 J.H.J.G.
C3 C.P.W.
C4 R.I.K.
C5 J.A.L.C.
D1 A.D.H.
D2 L.C.P.
D3 C.P.W.
D4 J.H.J.G.
D5 R.I.K.
E1 A.T.O.
E2 M.H.B.
E3 J.H.J.G.

FRENCH

A1 C. F. Dodd, Cerita, Marcham, nr. Abingdon
A2 R.St.J.Y.
A3 J.O.U.
A4 F.R.W.
A5 C.L.T.
B1 C.F.D.
B2 C.L.T.
B3 M. Milliken, St. Michael's School, E. Horsley, Surrey
B4 J.M.B.
B5 F.R.W.
C1 R.St.J.Y.
C2 C.L.T.
C3 M.M.
C4 F.R.W.
C5 J.O.U.
D1 C.F.D.
D2 J.O.U.
D3 J.M.B.
D4 M.M.
D5 R.St.J.Y.
E1 } C.F.D.
E2 }
E3 J.H.J.G.

DIVINITY: Rev. G. P. Wilkins, Church Hanborough, Oxon.
GEOGRAPHY: G. Denison-Smith, G. A. Barratt, M. J. Cooke.
ART: Miss K. R. Richardson, 114 Woodstock Road, Oxford.
SCIENCE: G. Sommerhoff, St. Clare, Ryde, I.o.W.
MUSIC: Miss M. Phipps, 41 Beech Croft Road, Oxford; Mrs. Senior, 34 Chalfont Road, Oxford; Miss M. Jones, St. James's Vicarage, Hatcham, London, S.E.14; Miss N. C. Bosanquet, Dingestow Court, Monmouth; Miss R. Schiele (O.D.), 3 Brookside, Headington, Oxford; Miss Woodward, 71 Brondesbury Road, London, N.W.6; A. E. Smith, 73A Observatory Street, Oxford.
HANDICRAFT: R. Barson, 7 Cranham Terrace, Oxford; Miss E. J. Houghton (Lowers).
CARPENTRY: R. G. Anderson, Dragon School, Oxford.
PHYSICAL TRAINING: J. C. Purnell, 13 Addison Crescent, Oxford.

BURSAR: E. L. Francis, 4 Garford Road, Oxford.

A great deal of information was given to parents about their children. The termly school magazine, the *Draconian*, would summarize the information about all of the pupils, including their age, weight and home addresses. That for my first term is as follows, where I can be seen in Lower V, with my address in Dorset.

Every two weeks the parents would be sent a fortnightly report, and at the end of term a fuller one. My final fortnightly report, commenting on the important Common Entrance exam, is as follows.

DRAGON SCHOOL FORTNIGHTLY REPORT

Name *Alan Macfarlane*   Age *13:6*   *10 July* 1955

	Form	No. of Boys in Form	Place last f'night	Place this f'night	Remarks
Classics	Up. 2B	17	=12	=13	good results in C.E. Exam. *(initials)*
English	A3	17	6	=8	Well done in C.E. J.A.T.
Mathematics	A2	18	=1	No places Well done. *(initials)*
French	A4	15	=2	=2	v.g. FLW
House					
School					good A.E.L.

The encouraging tone, notes on character and progress by the house and head master, show the care that was taken over the 400 or so pupils. My first termly report suggests that despite my rather miserable memories of that term, I may have not been suffering too much, since my work was praised, and though I was 'a quiet little person', I played rugger 'with incredible dash' and had 'settled down very well'.

DRAGON SCHOOL, OXFORD

In my last termly report I was getting enthusiastic comments on most subjects and my anxious (frowning) look of concentration was nearly gone. My 'zig zag' enthusiasm in swimming and impressive efforts in cricket were noted.

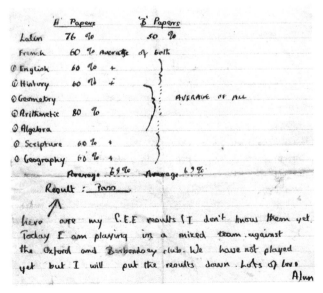

DRAGON SCHOOL, OXFORD

Name Alan Macfarlane Age 13.7   Terminal Report   JULY, 1955

Absent	/ days	Form	No. of Boys in Form	Place by Term's Marks	Place by Exam.	Remarks
Classics ...		Form Up 2B AV. AGE 13.4	17	13	11	He has made v.good progress with v.good exam to finish up. Best wishes. H.W.Mc.
English ...		Set A3 AV. AGE 13.0	17	=8 E =9 H =6		A very good term's work. Don't stop using your imagination in English. well done. S.A.S.
Mathematics ...		Set A2 AV. AGE 13.3	18	=1 V 4	4	A thoroughly good term's work HWS Good luck.
French ...		Set A4. AV. AGE 13.5	15	=3 V 5	5	A really good Term's work : well done ! P.E.W.
Geography ...		Set A3 A4	34	=10	12	Very good. J.P.

MUSIC AND SINGING		GAMES, P.T. ETC.— His batting improved enormously during the Term and I hope we will do really well later on. Canditory at my age a catch almost completed.
ART		Performed thoroughly well in the Sports.
HANDICRAFT ...	Good effort ARS	Swam with Zig-Zag enthusiasm in the 3rd Boat.
DIVINITY	5. v.g. H.W.A.G.	Did quite well as a drill-leader.
SCIENCE	Very satisfactory J.E.	

General Report (for Day-boys)—
House Report (for Boarders)— Alan has done very well all round, and the smile has nearly ousted the frown! But of late to him at Sedbergh. Jo

Headmaster's Report— Highly satisfactory— We all wish him a happy + useful Career.

A. E. LYNAM

Next Term begins Wednesday, September 21st, 1955, at 9.30 a.m.
Boarders return before 7.30 p.m. on the day before (Sept. 20th)   Holiday Prize Work :— Illustrated Holiday Diary
N.B.—No boy may return to School without a certificate of freedom from contact with infectious disorder during holidays

The results of all these efforts can be seen in the report I made to my parents on my 'Common Entrance' exams which allowed me to proceed to my public school. Reasonable in general, I am amazed to find that at that time I was good at mathematics.

	'A' Papers	'B' Papers
Latin	76 %	50 %
French	60 % Average of both	
① English	60 % +	
① History	60 % ÷	
① Geometry		AVERAGE OF ALL
① Arithmetic	80 %	
① Algebra		
① Scripture	60 % +	
① Geography	60 % +	
	Average 69%	Average 69%
Result :	Pass	

↑

here are my C.E.E results (I don't know them yet. Today I am playing in a mixed team against the Oxford and Berbondsey club. We have not played yet but I will put the results down. Lots of love
                                                                Alan

It is less easy to recall or document the content of our learning, though it is possible to show the standard and level of our work from examination papers. These, analysed in my fuller book on the Dragon, show that we were expected to be pretty competent in all our subjects.

Here I will just give two examples from the one set of school books I have kept, which were for the half-subject of geography, from the middle year of my schooling when I was between 11 and 12. The second is 'Prep' or preparation done in the evenings.

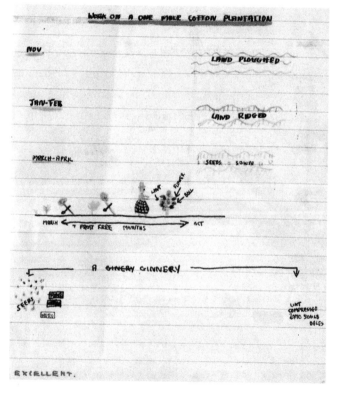

Prep

The central lowlands of Scotland

There are four main coalfields, the Lanark, Ayrshire, Midlothian and Fife coalfields. Glasgow is a great port but father further down stream down the Clyde there is the most famous shipbuilding area in the British Isles. Many ships of different kinds are built and launched. In Motherwell and Coatbridge iron and steel is manafactured. Many of the little fishing villages become holiday resorts in the summer.

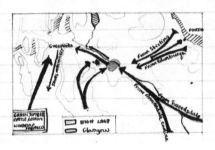

It is worth stressing that our education was meant to equip us with a good deal of more general knowledge. Each year there would be a test for the whole school. Here (overleaf) is the first half of one such test, which parents would be encourged to try to do also.

A Hundred General Knowledge Questions

[Answers and Report appear on a later page.]

[170 competitors. Number of correct answers given at end of each question.]

1. What writer created the character of Hercule Poirot? (54)
2. Who wrote the song ' Camptown Races? ' (7)
3. Where does a Novocastrian live? (20)
4. Whose collected works appeared in the First Folio? (37)
5. When the mother of Achilles dipped him in the river Styx what part of him did she hold on to? (79)
6. What ship was commanded by Capt. Corcoran? (13)
7. For what purpose does the Quorn exist? (4)
8. Who is the Earl Marshal of England? (27)
9. Who rode a horse called Swallow? (11)
10. What Shakespearian character said ' All the world's a stage '? (14)
11. What were Hitler's secret police called? (77)
12. Where did George Leigh Mallory meet his death? (29)
13. What do the letters W.S. stand for after the name of a Scottish solicitor? (0)
14. When was the next Derby winner born? (12)
15. What country is divided into Cantons? (18)
16. Who killed Carver Doone? (24)
17. Whose official residence is No. 11 Downing Street? (36)
18. What is a southpaw? (11)
19. What is the second book in the Bible? (62)
20. What famous Englishman became Duke of Bronte? (0)
21. What saint do you connect with the House of Commons? (7)
22. By what name is William Cody better known? (50)
23. What society was founded by George Fox? (11)
24. Who painted ' The Hay Wain '? (7)
25. In what unit do you express the height of a pony? (108)
26. Who is the Rector of Aberdeen University? (27)
27. Who is the Leader of the B.B.C. Symphony Orchestra? (15)
28. What does the prefix ' Tele-' mean? (40)
29. What letter in Morse code is three dots and a dash? (5)
30. Who made a speech at Gettysburg? (20)
31. Of what ' —ism ' would you be guilty if you referred to the American National Anthem as ' The Star-Bangled Spanner '? (7)
32. What is the more familiar term for Nostalgia? (3)
33. What vessel was wrecked on Raroia reef? (56)
34. What event is commemorated in France on July 14th? (28)
35. What title did Prince Charles acquire on the death of George VI? (66)
36. Whose hat, stuck on a pole, did William Tell refuse to acknowledge? (11)
37. What do the letters N.A.T.O. stand for? (32)
38. At what figure did the recent Budget fix the Food Subsidies? (5)
39. Where does the cross-channel service from New-haven sail to? (53)
40. Who is Chief of the Air Staff? (8)
41. What happens at Glyndebourne? (6)
42. What is the capital of Jugoslavia? (23)
43. Who said ' Guns will make us powerful: butter will only make us fat '? (1)
44. Who wrote ' Charley's Aunt '? (15)
45. Who discovered that Malaria is carried by mosquitoes? (3)
46. In what is a seismologist interested? (12)
47. Name the southernmost point in the Isle of Wight? (8)

An indirect indication of my process can also be seen from a small sample of the weekly letters I wrote to my parents, usually to India but in the first case, in my second term, to Dorset. The second letter, in the middle of my time, shows my new position in a dormitory in School House. Third was written after just arriving in Dorset, using a new pen and explaining my horror at a famous murder. My final letter from the school shows how I ended up.

TELEPHONE
OXFORD 47079

6 BARDWELL ROAD
OXFORD

27-3 1957

Dear mommy and Ann and froes,

I hope you are are better know after that flue. I love the comics and are enjoying your letters. Thank you very very much for the lovely sweets you sent me. The time is flying I am looking forward to the hols and Daddy coming

3/5/53

Dear Mummy and Dad Dad,
I have been at school for 2½ days so far. I am in a dorm called Pheonix wich is a big dorm and I am having jolly good fun. I played my first match yesterday, and I scored 5 not out. We had a lovely chaise yesterday of what to do. (A) we could see the Oxford University Athletics club have a competion against the Amateur England team and we could see people like bannister and Baily all afternoon or
(B) we could do that for an hour and then come back and see the Cup final on T.V. or
(C) Play cricket and watch the Cup final on B.T.V the sides

were Bolton Wanderers who had Englh Center Forward Nat Lofthouse and Englands Centre Ehulf M.Barass. Black Bo Blackpool had Stan Mortenson and and Stan Mathews. Blackpool 4 v Bolten 3. We are going to have a very good film tonight called "The Happiest Days of your life". Here is a sketch of our Dorm

That is Roughtly what it looks like Except Everything is closer toget lots of Love Alan

March 25th 1953

Dear Mummy and Daddy,
it was nice agetting back to By-the-way after a ha very pleasant term. There is a terrific gale blowing. I had a nice game of soccer this morning with Robert. Auntie Julia was very ill about three days ago by but she has gone to her mother now. I am enjoying the game of Monopoly you gave to me very much and I have played it 4 <u>times</u> already this hols. I have been rather frightened the last few nights as. A Mr Cristie has dissapeared from a place where a man knocked down the wall and found 5 women and the police dug up the garden and found two more women one of witch was Mrs Cristie. Granny has got about 36 brown chickens in a big house where they stay all the time and 44 white ones wich are in the same kind of

DRAGON SCHOOL
OXFORD

Friday

Dear Mr Mummy and Daddy,
I am so sorry as this letter will probabally not reach very soon but I think I might as well wait untill my results come and I have my papers back. I have played in three matches since Wednesday. Firstly I played against Cothill in which we won by about 70 runs I only made 8 runs but while I was in the score went from 44 for 5 to about 85. On Thursday I didn't bat against Cheltenham but we won by five wickets (They scored 100 98 for 7) and we scored 102 for 5). Yesterday there was 2nd II match against Salesian College. They declared (ra very decently) at 120 for 6. As someone was ill I was playing. Our first few batted well. Ellis 8 Scorah 14 Axtell 32. And when I went in it was 64 for 4. Then Exlson was out for 2. and Westrup came in. We began to look as if we would draw when by a fluke I hit 10 in 3 balls then Westrup hit 3 fours. But he was out for 25 but we managed to win with ten minutes to go. I made 33 not out.

The school was fully aware of the value of encouragements, so we all won certificates, book prizes and awards, particularly towards the end of our school time. Here is my prize for rugger and also the honorific 'Order of the Dragon' to show that I had completed my time at the school. By the end I thought of the place as paradise, and the leaver's photograph (where I am sixth from the right in the second row) found me very sad that it was all over. Many of the boys had become really close friends. I had grown in confidence and ability and was now 'prepared' for the next part of the journey, to a very different kind of school in the beautiful but harsh northern fells of Yorkshire.

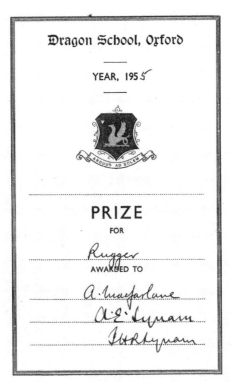

Dragon School, Oxford

YEAR, 1955

PRIZE

FOR

Rugger

AWARDED TO

a. macfarlane

a.e. lyman

JHRlyman

Alan Macfarlane

O. D. *July 1955.*

(ORDER OF THE DRAGON)

ARDUUS AD SOLEM

Others before self—
God before all.

A. E. Lynam

Jockynam.

FIVE

Living in the Lakes: 1954 – 1963

IN AUTUMN 1954 the family moved north for my last year at the Dragon School. My parents wanted to buy a house in northern England. My mother had fallen in love with the famous Lake District mountains and rivers where the great Romantic poets Wordsworth and Coleridge had lived. It would also be convenient for the Yorkshire boarding school to which I would hopefully go in late 1955.

We first moved to temporary accommodation to a house near Lake Windermere, from where my mother could search for houses. From Beck House, again shared with my grandparents, I went fishing in Lake Windermere and nearby tarns, carried on my obsession with model railways, and discovered the delights of tobogganing and walking up bracken covered mountains.

In the following spring my mother found the dream house they had been searching for, Field Head in the valley of Esthwaite Lake (marked on the map below above the letter 'S' of 'Hawkshead). Wordsworth had been to school in Hawkshead and the landscape was described in his autobiographical poem, 'The Prelude'. I would soon find myself consciously re-tracing his footsteps around the glorious countryside and later across the Continent.

The house itself was half of a seventeenth century farm-house, with a reasonable gardens, the front with a magnificent yew tree, and the back with apple trees and a small wooden shed which later became my first work room. My bedroom was a small oak-panelled room above the porch and I was to spend the next ten years in this room and exploring this area of outstanding beauty. In the old farm house over the garden wall, was a dilapidated farm house with a local farming family who became friends and whose eggs, dogs, horses and children enriched our lives. In that photograph the 'shed', my future first workroom, can be seen before it was converted.

There were glorious views down the valley to Hawkshead, along a path which I walked almost every week. The neighbouring mountains and particularly the famous Tarn Howes where I used to go to fish, swim and skate were inspiring. I walked extensively over most of the nearby mountains either alone or with friends and family and usually accompanied by a dog. Slightly further off was Lake Windermere, with its islands and associations, for me, with my childhood reading of 'Swallows and Amazons'.

Hawkshead was still a small market town, with an annual animal show to which my sister Fiona and I would take our dog 'Juno' to exhibit. It was dominated by a beautiful church where I was later to be married.

82373.   THE CHURCH & WORDSWORTH'S GRAMMAR SCHOOL, HAWKSHEAD.

Here, mostly in the company of my grandparents (my parents only coming home on leave for a few months every two or three years) my sisters and I grew from childhood, through adolescence into early adulthood.

My mother remained emotionally the centre of my life, however, through her constant letters, encouragement and creative imagination. Despite a polio damaged leg she accompanied us on expeditions when she was home on leave, and energised our lives from her seat in the drawing room of Field Head.

My still bachelor schoolmaster uncle Richard was also important, walking with me, playing music, discussing books and taking me on religious boys camps.

My uncle Robert, a key influence in my Dorset Days, had now left home. He went to Oxford around the time we moved north and then became a Clerk in the House of Commons and married Angela, so only occasionally visited us. The oldest uncle,

Billy, we saw very little of as he had retired from the army and also become a schoolmaster and married Julia.

One of my main outdoor activities was walking and exploring
the hills and lakes around us, a passion which overlapped with
similar walking around the hills of my nearby school at Sedbergh. I did this in all weathers, either alone or with my family.

My greatest passion, however, was fishing for trout, with fly and worm, and occasionally for sea-trout (the bridge above which I caught my first sea trout on the Duddon is below). I approached the matter scientifically both at home and at school. Particularly important was a small beck (stream) running just below our house called Black Beck. I caught many trout there, which surprised me on my return fifty years later when the stream seemed to have shrunk from that of my memories.

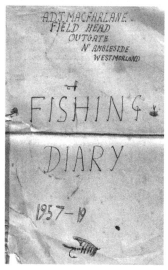

DATE	Height	PLACE	NOS	SIZE
17/3/57	7½	Pools on Rawthey 5(2) :–1(1)	3	6½, 7, 6½ ins.
21/3/57	7½	Pool on Rawthey –2 (3)	3 [1]	8½", 7½, 7½ ins.
22/3/57	7	Pool " –2(1) : 5(2)	3	6, 5½, 5½ ins.
24/3/57	6	Pool " = 6(1) 5(1) 2(4)	6 [1]	8½, 7½, 6½, 6½, 6, 5m.
29/3/57	5	Pool " – 4 p¹⁰ below Red Bridge	1 [2]	5 "
29/3/57	5	Black Beck [Above Bridge]	4 [3]	between 4½ – 6½ in'
29/3/57	4	Rydal Beck	15 [2]	"
3/4/57	4	Brathay [below br –t. where it goes into lake]	1 [1]	7½ " [" "]
5/4/57	3	Langdale beck [Saw small grey dun]	5 [0]	4", 3½" , 4" 3 in"
11/4/57	3	Rydal Beck – Scandal Beck		
23/4/57	4½	Brathay – just above br	0 [0]	
25/4/57	4	Black Beck	2 [0]	6¾ 5½
2/5/57	4½	Pool on Rawthey +2 (2)+3(1)+6(2) +10(1)	7 [1]	8, 7½, 6, 6, 6, 5, c
4/5/57	4	" " +3(4)+6(2)	6 [1]	9½ 7½, 6½, 6, 6, 6 ins
5/5/57	4	" below Lords Dub+3(1)4(5)+5(1)	7 [9]	10½, 6½ 7, 6 6, 5½, 2½ ins
6/5/57	4	" just above New Bridge (10)	10 [2]	9, 8½ 6, 7, 6½, 6, 5½, 5,5
12/5/57		Above Danny bridge sp (Clough	4 [1]	5, 6, 5, 7½ ins
13/5/57	3	Above New Br Rocky pools – Clough	2 (0)	6,6, ins
14/5/57	6	" " "	2 (1)	9,6 ins
16/5/57	6	" " pls 1, 2, 3.	0 0	6 0 ins
22/5/57	5	" " " "	3 (0)	3, 6, 7½ ins
24/5/57	4	Up Rawthey St M.S. opp.	9 (4)	9½, 9, 8½, 8¼, 7,6,5,5 ins (cont')
26/5/57	4	" 2m ½ up to bel St M.S.	13 (6)	9½, 8 8¾, 8½, 8¼, 8 ½ ins
31/5 /57	3½	Hebblethwaite – ½ mile up to	16 (3)	8½, 7½, 7½, 7, 7–3½ in
1/6 /57	2¼	Rawthey up to ½ mile Hebbthwt	6 (2)	8, 7½, 4½ .4½, 3,3,0
2/6/57	3	Above Lords Dub – Jackdaw	2 (2)	9½, 9 in'

The sea on the Cumberland coast was a few hours drive away, but the trip was usually enlivened by stopping in the beautiful Duddon valley. Picnics were also a high point in these expeditions.

My other increasing hobby, alongside the motorbike I bought at sixteen, was the whole 'pop' or popular music scene, which coincided with the advent of 'Rock 'n Roll'. These were the years of Elvis Presley, Buddy Holly and Lonnie Donegan, and I bought my first guitar and hung out with better players in coffee shops and strummed to my family.

It was over the Christmas season of my 18th birthday that I entered the party scene and found my first girl friend, and also became friends with other girls in the neighbourhood. Here at a party are many of my friends and myself and my first girl-friend on the bottom left. Through the sociable nature of my grandmother, our home became a centre of the social life of this part of the Lake District and friends from the Dragon school who lived nearby (back right) and from Sedbergh (with large girl on his knees) were among 'the gang'.

We went to Scotland several times during these years, and particularly memorable was a fishing holiday in the Orkneys with my father. In the winter of 1958, over my 17th birthday, my sisters went out to Assam for the winter holidays. We spent a month, camping and fishing up the Manas river on the border of Bhutan. Memories of this were later behind my desire to return to work in the Himalayas.

Some eight months after the trip to India, my closest friend at Sedbergh and I decided to hitch-hike around Europe. Our route followed as closely as possible that of William Wordsworth on his tour just before the French Revolution. My aim was to try to see what had changed, and whether I could throw any light on some of his experiences, particularly a moment of high poetic emotion on the Simplon Pass between Italy and Switzerland. I drew the route for my parents and I presented my account to Oxford University for a Trevelyan Scholarship.

At the end of my time at school I had six months free before going to University. In this 'gap' half year I went to Norway where I worked on a cargo boat between Bergen and Amsterdam, lightening what was otherwise a rather traumatic (sea, home and love sick simultaneously) time, by playing football for the boat team. After that I worked for a few months in a bakery and with money from these jobs I was able to buy a small sailing boat which we kept on Lake Windermere, and is below being rowed by the younger sister of my first girl-friend.

These ten years in the Lakes, complementing the five years at school in Yorkshire were a refreshing contrast to my life in the south of England, in Dorset and the Dragon, and later as an undergraduate and postgraduate at Oxford from 1960. They were an almost perfect home environment in which to move through puberty. Although I missed my parents very much, my grandmother helped me to launch into wider society and my friendships, especially with girls, took me out into a broader world.

The times in the Lakes were largely to rest and recover from the strain of the hard work of school and later University. At school I do not remember any home work, apart from a little reading, being set, so most of my time was free. From university I started to work at home and turned my little room, and then the renovated 'shed' in the garden into a library and writing room.

My sisters were my closest companions of my own age and with them I went through the transition from the still somewhat austere and conventional England of 1954 when we moved north, to the world of the early Beatles and increasing affluence. A straw in the wind on which this account can end, is in a letter from my sister to my parents in India on 11 Jan 1957. Fiona wrote

> *Do tell me what "Rock about the Clock" is like. There are lots of Rocking tunes but I think the one in it is "1 oclock 2 oclock 3 oclock ROCK!" There is a Teddy Boy in Hawkshead. He wears black shiny trousers which get higher at the bottom with elastic and bright green socks and a sort of old-fashioned hair. I've seen him twice!*

Even in remotest Hawkshead the new world had arrived.

SIX

Sedbergh School
1955 – 1960

FOLLOWING MY THREE maternal uncles, I went to Sedbergh, a boarding school in the Yorkshire moors at the age of thirteen and three quarters. I remained there for nearly five years. Again it was difficult at first, but the glorious scenery, including rivers and fells, and some excellent teachers and developing friendships made it more than tolerable and by the end I was through puberty and really excited by ideas. I gained a place at Oxford University for 1960.

The school was set between several mountains up which we ran, and was surrounded by four rivers, the largest being the salmon river the Lune, as shown in my map to my parents, which also gives the course of the two important cross country races, the Three Mile up the Dee river and the Ten Mile up the Rawthey.

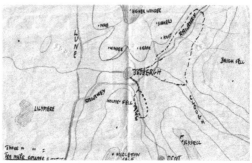

The school had been founded in 1525, but it was extensively extended and new buildings were added, including seven boarding houses as well as playing fields, in the later nineteenth century. My house, Lupton, is marked 2 on the map, near the top. It was unusual in being just an ordinary house, situated on the edge of the town, and hence felt less oppressive. Other key points, including the swimming bath, tuck shop, sanatorium and chapel are shown on the map provided for us at the time.

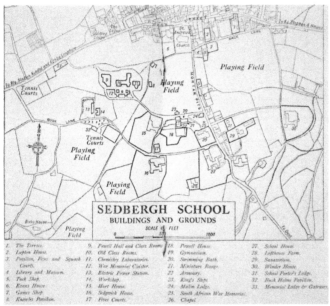

The school provided a framework for our lives. For example there were rules about where we should go and what we should do, both at the level of the school and of the house. The first page of these rules shows how we were to a certain extent hemmed in. This also applied to our clothing, which was not only carefully prescribed, but had to be worn in particular ways depending on our age and status in the school.

J. OWEN

SCHOOL RULES

GENERAL RULES.

1. Boys are forbidden to use or possess pistols of any description, catapults or similar playthings, gunpowder, fireworks or cartridges.

2. All breakages or damages, whether of School or other property, must be at once reported, in Houses to the Housemaster, elsewhere to the Headmaster.

3. Betting, raffling, sweepstakes and the like, and the use or possession of playing cards are forbidden.

4. All books used in School below the Sixth Form, except Bibles and books drawn from House stores, must bear the owner's name stamped on them by the School Bookseller.

5. No boy may obtain credit from any tradesman, and no eatables may be obtained on parents' standing order without Housemaster's consent.

6. No alcoholic drinks may be brought into a House; no boy may enter a Hotel or Public House without written leave from his Housemaster.

7. The use or possession of smoking materials is forbidden.

8. No boy may go beyond his House Yard after tea without written leave, except to the fields and courts in the Summer Term

9. Written leave from Housemasters is required for any form of transport. No boy may drive a motor vehicle, nor keep one in or near Sedbergh.

10. The School Shop is out of bounds except as under :— Winter Terms, Whole School days 3-20—4-15 p.m. Half-holidays 3-40—6-15 p.m. Summer Term, Whole School days 4-30—6-30 p.m. Half-holidays 4—6-30 p.m. On extra Holidays 2—2-30 p.m. (for purchase of chocolate and biscuits only) and 5—6-30 p.m. On their way to the Range boys may enter the Shop to purchase chocolate and biscuits between 2—2-30 p.m.

11. All impositions, including turned work, must be done on imposition paper, and must be signed by the boy's Housemaster before being shown up. They must be done at the earliest available opportunity, but not on Sunday, in preparation, or when a boy is due for afternoon exercise, N.R.R., C.M.I., Band or Choir practice.

HOUSE RULES.

12. Eatables are not allowed in Dormitories.

13. No nails may be driven into the walls of studies or cubicles.

SEDBERGH SCHOOL
CLOTHES LIST

Name ....

Minimum number required	ARTICLES IN DETAIL	Number sent	Number returned
1	PAIR GREY FLANNELS OR KILT	1	
1	TWEED JACKET (Blue Grey, Grey or Lovat)	1	
1	PULLOVER (one quiet colour)	1	
2	WHITE SHIRTS (not collar attached)	3	
3	WHITE VAN HEUSON OR SIMILAR COLLARS	2	
2	BLACK NECK TIES	2	
2	PAIRS THIN SOCKS (for Sundays)	2	
* 2	BLUE BLAZERS	2	
* 2	PAIRS BLUE SHORTS	3	
† 2	WHITE SWEATERS (V-necked)	2	
* 3	BLUE SHIRTS	4	
* 3	PAIRS BLUE STOCKINGS	3	
2	PAIRS GARTERS	2	
3	VESTS	3	
3	PAIRS PANTS	3	
3	PAIRS PYJAMAS	3	
12	HANDKERCHIEFS	12	
1	RAINCOAT	1	
1	GREATCOAT (optional in summer)		
1	DRESSING GOWN	1	
1	PAIR DARK LEATHER SLIPPERS	1	
2	PAIRS BLACK SHOES	2	
1	HAIR BRUSH	2	
1	COMB	1	
1	SPONGE OR FACE CLOTH	1	
6	BATH TOWELS (medium size with TAG FOR HANGING)		
1	RUG		
6	SHEETS		
3	PILLOW CASES		

FOR GAMES (in addition to above)

* 2	BROWN FOOTBALL JERSEY	2	
* 2	BLUE FOOTBALL JERSEY	2	
* 2	PAIRS FOOTBALL SHORTS	3	
* 3	PAIRS BROWN FOOTBALL STOCKINGS	2	
3	PAIRS GREY SOCKS (thick for running or cricket)		
1	PAIR GREY FLANNELS (for cricket)		
3	WHITE SHIRTS, LONG-SLEEVED (for summer term)		
1	PAIR BATHING TRUNKS		
† 1	PAIR FOOTBALL BOOTS (for winter term)	1	
† 1	PAIR WHITE GYM SHOES	1	
† 1	PAIR CRICKET BOOTS OR SHOES (for summer term)		

* To be obtained in School shop by New Boys at beginning of term.
† Available in School shop.

NOTES

N.B. (1) **Each article**, including Greatcoats and Rugs, must be marked with the initials, full surname and House of the boy, on woven name tapes (such as Cash's). At least two dozen extra name tapes for matron's use should also be sent.

(2) Each article must be brought **clean** and in **good repair** at the beginning of each term.

(3) Each boy must have a solid label to his keys, with his name upon it, and must bring a suitcase or handbag large enough to contain a suit. This suitcase should be marked with name or initials.

2,000. 11. 57.

When we arrived we spent the first couple of weeks learning all the rules, the school songs, and where all the different runs across the country went. The numerous runs, their names, distance, average times, were written, as in the following.

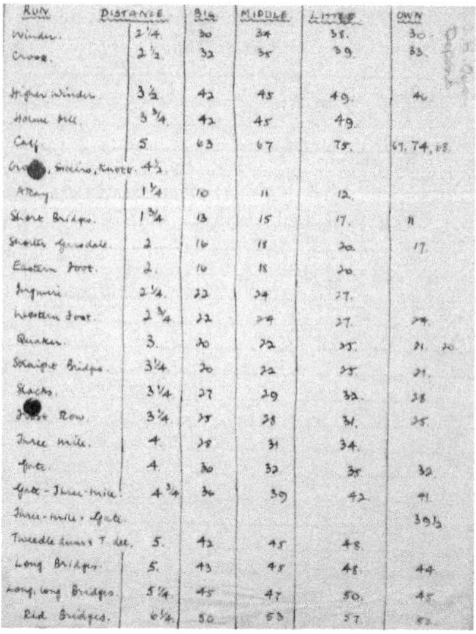

Run	Distance	Big	Middle	Little	Own
Winder.	2¼	30	34	38.	30.
Cross.	2½.	32	35	39.	33.
Higher Winder	3½	42	45	49.	46
Holme Hill.	3¾.	42	45	49.	
Calf.	5.	63	67	75.	67, 74, 68.
Cro[illegible], [illegible], Knott.	4½.				
A Ray.	1¼.	10	11	12.	
Short Bridges.	1¾	13	15	17.	11
Shorter Garsdale.	2.	16	18	20.	17.
Eastern Front.	2.	16	18	20.	
Ingmire.	2¼.	22	24	27.	
Western Front.	2¾.	22	24	27.	24.
Quaker.	3.	20	22	25.	21. 20
Straight Bridges.	3¼	20	22	25.	21.
Stacks.	3¼	27	29	32.	28
[illegible] Row.	3¼.	25	28	31.	25.
Three mile.	4.	28	31	34.	
Gate.	4.	30	32	35	32.
Gate - Three-mile.	4¾	36	39	42.	41.
Three-mile - Gate.					39½
Tweedle dums & T. dee.	5.	42	45	48.	
Long Bridges.	5.	43	45	48.	44
Long, long Bridges.	5¼.	45	47	50.	45.
Red Bridges.	6¼.	50	53	57.	52.

The induction into the school (motto – 'A Hard Nurse of Men') was tough, with muddy games, cold baths every morning, running up mountains and snowball fights through the icy bitter lanes. There was little privacy (even baths were shared) and a new set of customs to learn.

Yet this extract from my diary for the second term, the worst of the year, suggests that I was surviving and even doing reasonably in class. The diary mentions the start of the fishing season, and from the first I spent much of my leisure time thinking about the trout in the river Rawthey just below the school.

MARCH, 1956	MARCH, 1956
11 SUNDAY 4th in Lent	**15 THURSDAY** Went round ex higher Winder nab, horrible day the weather was clouded over
12 MONDAY ● New Moon I was 1st in fortnight. Went round ex Flostross. Lovely day should have been extra.	**16 FRIDAY** Fishing season starts it snowed a bit! played yard v Winder we beat them 13-3. Three mile trials.
13 TUESDAY Went on fells, as it is off day retrieved my reel from Hebbelthwaite. Jarvis did 10 in 1hr 33 not bad.	**17 SATURDAY** S. Patrick Bank Holiday in Eire and Northern Ireland Boxing finals, played yard
14 WEDNESDAY Played yard v Winder beat them. French 9-5. French bits out of 30 Went to Father Hanks' address. The organ worked.	**NOTES** I am 1st on Report order

As the summer arrived everything improved and instead of having to race up Winder just north of the town, we could play cricket or go for expeditions across the glorious fells.

By far our most important social and psychological world was provided by the boarding house. Each house had about fifty boys, divided into year groups in accomodation, dormitories, eating tables, teams and privileges. In this group photograph taken in my third year (I am in the third row up, third from the right) there are several important figures. The housemaster and assistant housemaser, with the housemaster's wife and house matron and the house prefects are in the second row. The little boys who acted as servants ('fags') were in the first row. The single school cup won by the house that year is symbolically in the middle.

The house order in the 'Brown Book' followed the class ordcer in the school. That for my last term shows me in capitals as a school prefect. The list was read out each evening to check all boys were back in the house.

LUPTON HOUSE				HART HOUSE	
		IVc.	R. S. Gilchrist		
			Morrison		
U.VI.C.	*M. T. Sykes		I. R. Thompson	U.VI.C.	*Balderston
	*Magee		Byles?		Bird
U.VI.M.a.	*M. J. P. Vignoles		Sheldon	U.VI.M.a.	*J. F. Hamilton
	Peel	IVd.	Somerville	U.VI.M.b.	P. Cook
	†G. L. Bromley		Mercer		Mann
U.VI.M.b.	P. J. S. Watson	IIIa.	M. J. Scott	Clio.	Page
	I. S. W. Hall	IIIb.	Jamieson?		BUSTARD
	Kay		Liptrott	M.L.VI.	Halliwell
	Highton	IIa.	P. J. Donald		Sugden
	Oliver		Stout		Townley
	CAMPBELL		Caton		Gairdner
	†Hunter	IIb.	F. S. Henderson	Bio.VI.	†Williams
Clio.	A. D. J. MACFARLANE				*Burgess
	*†C. H. Vignoles		(58)		†W. B. Graham
	Bland				†Metcalfe-Gibson
	Porter			Gen.VI.	†Bagshaw
M.L.VI.	Black				Tinniswood
Bio.VI.	R. G. H. Savory			L.VI.C.	Cross
L.VI.C.	*N. W. A. Scott				R. A. Sheard
L.VI.M.b.	Knox				W. K. Wood
	B. J. Bromley			L.VI.M.a.	*Davidson
	†A. Barnes				J. R. Rhind
L.VI.H.	*M. W. Scott			L.VI.M.b.	Aitchison
	Rink				E. M. Sykes
	R. E. G. W. Robinson				Rocke
Va.C.	*R. H. Vignoles				Teasdale
	Grierson		E. M. Sheard	Va.C.	*Pirie
Va.M.	Bannister		*Mungall		J. C. Smith
	Gates		Worters		Mawdsley
	Milne	IVb.	Anderson		Openshaw
	P. N. Gilchrist	IVc.	Vaillant	Vb.C.	Templer
Vb.M.	J. R. Smith	IVd.	Hand		Goddard
	Mason		Espley		Maxwell
	P. A. Thomson		Partington		Scales
	J. G. S. Donald		Maingay	Va.M.	*M. F. Smith
	D. A. Donald		Lydall		I. C. Gray
	S. L. Graley		Ogden		Burnett
IVa.	*More	IIIb.	Crossley		M. J. C. Harrison
	*M. S. Graley?		James		Hyde
	Martin		Stacpoole	Vb.M.	L. R. Dawson
IVb.	Rabagliati		Owen		Greenwood
	Rich	IIb.	I. L. H. Harrison		Holmes
	Gardner				Blakemore
	Brigham		(61)	IVa.	Murtland
					*Downie

The house was largely run through power delegated to the house prefects, just as the school was run by the school prefects, a couple per house, shown having a meeting (overleaf) in the headmaster's study.

The prefects exercised most of their authority through word of mouth and example, reporting any difficulties to the house or head master. But they also had powers to inflict punishments. The major form of punishment was beating, up to six strikes with a slipper. This had to be approved and noted in a book by the housemaster. A minor punishment was to set a boy a task, for example to draw and colour in a certain number of maps with specified numbers of words on them. I avoided beating any boy and was, to my memory, only beaten once or twice at the most. But I did set some maps and punished others by making them do something useful like tidying up the house library.

At the top of the house were the three 'Senior Prefects', including the head of house. Here is my uncle Robert celebrating his power, some eight years before I was to occupy exactly the same study. No doubt they are the same curtains and the there is the same bell on the wall to summon the 'fags' to make us toast or fetch our boots.

Moving after two years from the Junior and Senior Day Rooms, which one shared with a dozen or more boys and only had a small locker, to a study, which one shared with two or three others was a turning point. The luxury of space, pictures of girls, a fire for which one could chop wood in the back yard, began to tell us that we were becoming people of importance and moving from childhood to adult status. (The photograph, from the 1930's, show the boys wearing old-fashioned leggings. They are also wearing the characteristic short trousers which we wore every week-day through my time at Sedbergh).

We spent a good deal of our leisure time when the weather was reasonable either sitting and chatting, or playing volun-tary games in the school yard on the other side of the small back road. We also had a small common room open to all boys, another example of the club room which I had first encoun-tered at the Dragon and would end up inhabiting in the shape of an Oxbridge Common Room.

This was a world which our parents seldom penetrated. Being in India for most of my school time, they only took me out out three or four times. We would try to have a picnic or go to a local hotel. Only once did they come to eat toast in my study.

The house bound us together and taught us the values of loyalty, comradeship, friendship and hierarchy. A prize united us, as when my uncle Billy brought back this cup with a friend. And we 'ragged' in various ways, including making human mountains on the fells, or went with our best friends to climb a local mountain (Alan on the right).

INGLEBOROUGH.

The friendships of leisure were cemented by various team and joint sports which were at the centre of life.

The one feature of all this that is very obvious is the absence of girls. We had our sisters and other females relatives, but in the monastic existence of the school at that time, apart from a very occasional dance with a local girl's school, there was no chance to encounter girls. It thus struck me as a particular irony to find, when I returned 50 years later, that my house had been turned into the first girl's house in what is now a co-educational school, with young ladies such as this as pupils.

Our intellectual schooling occupied every morning except Sunday, but all afternoons were devoted to outdoor activities. On three days this lasted a couple of hours, the other three days we did not go back after lunch. The two formal and most highly regarded school games were rugger and cricket. Rugger was the supreme game of endurance and skill and I was at first promising, but never achieved the success of reaching the first fifteen, unlike my uncles Billy and Richard, both of whom had been good players. Richard's team (Richard seated centre right) won a prize for Lupton some twenty years before I went to the school. But I was just one of those who went out practicing and moving through the middle ranks.

Nor did I distinguish myself at cricket, a game which competed with my desire to go trout fishing through the summer term. Again my uncles 20 years earlier had been more success-ful at this game.

The other greatly valued sport was running. It was believed to teach stamina and tenacity, and to give us a sound body in which to keep our sound mind and pure spirit. The great sweep of the mountains provided a platform for runs which happened two or three times a week all through the two winter terms.

The peak of this activity was the challenging ten-mile race, which started outside our house and roared down Back Lane (my friend Alan Barnes in the lead), then went across punishing hills and muddy slides, (my friend Jamie Bruce Lockhart on the right), and ended up outside the school Tuck Shop, where (my uncle Richard is coming in third). Again, I was never much good at this and found all the running somewhat stressful and tedious, though I loved walking the same paths.

My outdoor passion revolved around the rivers rather than the mountains. In particular, as in the Lake District, I spent much of my energy thinking about and practicing trout fishing. We would get a licence which gave us permission to fish along three of the local rivers and I came to know every yard of these, making small maps to show where the fish lay and keeping careful logs of what I had caught, with what bait, where.

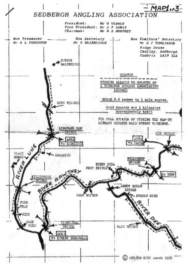

FISHING (Summer '58)

April 29 2(t) 4(all) - (fly) - Mid Raw - 10ins.
7 May 5th 3(t) 6(all) - (worm) Up Raw - Eff-s.
May 20th - (Rawthey) - (spinner) -
May 22nd 5(t) 10(all) - Blue Quill - Up Rawthey, 9-6
May 24th - (line) - - - (spinner)
May 28th - - (line) - (worm) - 7-8½
June 1st 6(t) - Clough - Blue quill ½ - 1mile.
June 3rd 16(t) - 11(all) - Clough Blue red quill.
June 7th 6(t) - 12(all) - Cl - Blue+red quill - 10"
7 June 10th 4(t) - 4(all) - Cl (Mitt) - Gr Quill -
June 14th 3(t) - 3(all) - Raw - New br - Greger
June 20th 2(t) - 3(all) - Raw - 2½ bigpt - 12½, 9"
June 25th 8(t) - 3(all) - Cl - Mitt-quill 10"
6 July 5th - 0 - 3(all) - spoon - Dee - not very good
5 July 6th - 4 - 11(all) worm - Raw (4#) - 7-8½"
4 July 8th - - - - worm for Sea-tr line.
3½ July 10 10(t) - 10(all) - worm up Raw 1½-4-9½,
4 July 13 8(t) - 9(all) - worm up Raw - 2" - 5 - 8½.

-# = up to Penny bridge.

I had friends who were able to catch salmon in the Lune, though I never did so, but my life was enriched by the magic of fishing through the summers, and preparing in fly-tying classes in the winter.

My other summer delight was swimming, particularly in the Lune, where we would go for blissful afternoons, again looking for salmon.

Fishing and swimming had to be suspended occasionally for cricket, and again for a couple of weeks at the time of competitive atheletics towards the end of the summer term. Fortunately I was small and slow and not much good at this either, so I did not have to spend much time on the high jump, hurdles or discus throwing.

Again, as at the Dragon and in the Lakes, what I enjoyed most in the winter was skating, which we did on several small lakes (tarns) a short distance from the school.

Less appealing, though quite central to our school life, was participation from our second year in military training. From the middle of the nineteenth century public schools had been seen as places where young men should be trained for fighting, in case of a war, and hence Sedbergh had a Combined Cadet Force. We would shine our buckles and polish our boots, learn to fire guns and march around. Once a year we engaged in a large mock battle on 'Field Day'. I never rose high up the ranks and found playing with very ancient and out of date military equipment only mildly enjoyable.

We were encouraged as much as possible to learn the various performance arts, as we had been at the Dragon. There was only occasionally Shakespeare or Gilbert and Sullivan, but houses would perform plays or, in one case, a mock trial for the rest of the boys and I took part in one of these. They caught the various romantic and contemporary (Teddy Boys) topics of the time, as the second 'Mock Trial' photograph shows. And of course, boys had to play the girls. In the end of term concerts which each house performed for itself we were allowed to poke fun at school life and even our teachers (within limits).

We were also encouraged to make music in our own houses. Here we have the jazz band started up in School House during my time, which I paralleled in a skiffle group which I helped to start up in Lupton in my third year. My group performed in public at a school fete and in the end of term concerts.

The school was, in fact, very musical, partly reflecting the enthusiasm of the headmaster. We heard many concerts in the school hall, including recitals by international soloists and world famous orchestras. Each house was also filled with music alongside the pop music coming from the studies, with gramaphone clubs and inter-house music competitions.

It is not surprising that Lupton won the inter-house competition for the Quartet since two of the four became international soloists later in their lives. (The capitals are the houses – W for Winder, L for Lupton and so on. And the numbers re the totals we scored).

SEDBERGH SCHOOL

INTER-HOUSE MUSIC COMPETITIONS
(Singing)

in

POWELL HALL

on

WEDNESDAY, 27th MARCH, 1957
at 7.30 p.m.

Judge:
FREDERIC H. WOOD, Esq., Mus.Doc.

QUARTETS:

W	House 'A'	'So fare thee well'	Brahms
H	House 'B'	'Never weather-beaten sail'	Campion
E	House 'C'	'Since first I saw your face'	Ford
S.H	House 'D'	'Early one morning'	Trad. arr. Dunhill
P	House 'E'	'Clorinda false'	Morley
L	House 'F'	'If ye love Me keep my commandments'	Tallis
S	House 'G'	'O stay, sweet love'	Farmer

NOS

UNISON SONGS:

E	House 'A'	(a) 'Had a horse'	Hungarian, arr. Korbay
		(b) 'Twelve oxen'	Warlock
	House 'B'	(a) Part of 'An Die Ferne Geliebte'	Beethoven
		(b) 'The Plough-boy'	Trad. arr. Britten
L	House 'C'	(a) 'Sea Fever'	Ireland
		(b) 'Oh, I've got plenty of nuttin'	Gershwin
P	House 'D'	(a) 'Love triumphant'	Brahms
		(b) 'The roadside fire'	Vaughan Williams
H	House 'E'	(a) Psalm 139 (v. 1-13) with Gloria	Plainsong
		(b) 'The road to the Isles'	Hebridean, arr. Kennedy Fraser
S.H	House 'F'	(a) 'Serenade'	Schubert
		(b) 'Pretty Polly Perkins'	Trad. arr. Clifton
S	House 'G'	(a) 'The miller's flowers'	Schubert
		(b) 'The vagabond'	Vaughan Williams

177
164
171
165
178
167
166

PLACES

Titus Wilson, Kendal

We were also encouraged in ;ublic speaking, with several debating and discussion societies. These were well attended and I can be seen (bottom right) listening attentively to a (staged) debate. This was again necessary preparation in case, later, we became lawyers, politicians, academics or others who would need to have rhetorical skills. One of my triumphs was as a Conservative political candidate in a mock election, where I swept the board – not surprising amongst a conservative set of boys.

There were many other societies and clubs. Some of them studied natural history and birds. Others collected fossils for the museum, named after the founder of British geology and an old boy of the school, Adam Sedgwick.

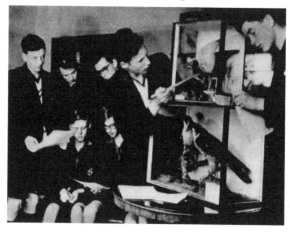

The previous headmaster had been a good painter, and the school had built up a lively art centre. I enjoyed painting in water colour and though I was undistinguished, a number of my friends became good artists. We were also encouraged to practice crafts, not just fly tying but also pottery, wood carving and book binding with a local binder.

The school was re-founded by Henry Hart, a pupil of the great mid-nineteenth century reformers of public schools, Arnold, Temple and Vaughan, in the attempt to make young men not only gentlemen, but Christian gentlemen. So religion was a central part of Sedbergh and I went through my most devout phase here.

I was confirmed into the Anglican church, went on religious boys camps and, like everyone else, went to services in the school Chapel every week, listened to many sermons, and said prayers before the start of each day and each meal. My time at Sedbergh was considerably affected by my desire to reconcile my desire to be spiritually pure and to believe in a saving Christ, along with doubts about the problems of pain and other religions, and attempts to master what I was told was my own sinfulness.

With all these threads to be woven together, to which needs to be added the meals, the sleeping, the preparations for lessons and the lessons themselves, it was a hectic life. We suffered home-sickness, illness, cold and hunger, but we were seldom bored.

And the way in which the events were strung together is well illustrated in the calendar for just one term of my life in the school, which also shows the heavy influence of formal religion, the importance of prizes and competitions, the debates and visiting speakers, and the ever present army parades. The annotations by me show the events which I needed to report on as editor of the school magazine (Sedberghian) and house magazine (Luptonian) in this my last term at the school.

CALENDAR

Holy Communion every Sunday at 8-15.
Sunday Morning Service at 11-0.   Sunday Evening Service at 6-30.
Saints' days: Holy Communion in the Parish Church 7-30 a.m.

JANUARY.

Fri.	15	Term begins. Master of the week: Mr. Forster.
Sat.	16	Chapel at 9 a.m.
S.	17	Second Sunday after Epiphany. Preacher: The Headmaster.
Mon.	18	Master of the week: Mr. Boggis. Lock-up 5-15 p.m.
Tues.	19	Weech Junior History.
Wed.	20	Parade.
Thurs.	21	
Fri.	22	Civics at 8-0 p.m. J. F. M. Doogan, Esq., on "Brathay".
Sat.	23	
S.	24	Third Sunday after Epiphany. Preacher: The Rev. A. T. I. Boggis.
Mon.	25	St. Paul. Master of the week: Mr. Hammer. Comers and Leavers lists to the Headmaster. Careers Talk: 8-30 p.m.
Tues.	26	Latin Prose Prize.
Wed.	27	Parade. Recital by the Northern Consort: 8 p.m. (in Chapel).
Thurs.	28	
Fri.	29	Wakefield French Prizes. Civics at 8 p.m. H. B. Creighton, Esq., on "Motorways".
Sat.	30	1st Fortnight's Orders. Lock-up 5-45 p.m. Debating Society.
S.	31	Fourth Sunday after Epiphany. Preacher: The Rev. A. J. W. Barker, Warden of Scargill House, Kettlewell.

FEBRUARY.

Mon.	1	Master of the week: Mr. Gairdner. Careers Talk: 8-30 p.m.
Tues.	2	Presentation of Christ in the Temple. VIth Form Literature Prize.
Wed.	3	
Thurs.	4	Double Parade.
Fri.	5	
Sat.	6	VIth Form Reports. 1st XV v. Catterick Services (H).
S.	7	Fifth Sunday after Epiphany. Preacher: The Rev. Canon R. T. Holtby, Director of Religious Education in Diocese of Carlisle.
Mon.	8	Master of the week: Mr. Long.
Tues.	9	Greek Verse Prize. Civics at 8 p.m. Miss D. Sylvester on "Counties in Danger".
Wed.	10	Parade.
Thurs.	11	
Fri.	12	Rankin Shakespeare.

Sat.	13	2nd Fortnight's Orders. Subscription Concert 8 p.m. 1st XV v. Bradford Grammar School (A).
S.	14	Septuagesima. Holy Communion 8-15 and 11-40. Preacher: The Rev. M. H. Bates, Vicar of Great Crosby, Liverpool.
Mon.	15	Master of the week: Mr. Morgan. Concert by the New English Orchestra, 8 p.m.
Tues.	16	
Wed.	17	Danson Science Prize. Parade.
Thurs.	18	Lecture by George B. Spenceley, Esq., F.R.G.S., on "South Georgia", 8 p.m.
Fri.	19	
Sat.	20	VIth Form Reports. Debating Society. 1st XV v. Newcastle Royal Grammar School (H).
S.	21	Sexagesima. Preacher: The Rev. T. A. Harman.
Mon.	22	Master of the week: Mr. Alban. Evans Divinity Prize, VIth Forms. Common Entrance Examination.
Tues.	23	Common Entrance Examination. 1st XV v. Northern F.C. (H)
Wed.	24	St. Matthias.
Thurs.	25	Double Parade.
Fri.	26	
Sat.	27	3rd Fortnight's Orders. A Running VIII v. Ampleforth (A).
S.	28	Quinquagesima. No sermon.
Mon.	29	Master of the week: Mr. Mills.

MARCH.

Tues.	1	Shrove Tuesday. Fives: first round. Entertainment by Herbert Milton 8 p.m.
Wed.	2	Ash Wednesday. Holy Communion 7-30 a.m. Service in the Chapel 9 a.m. Voluntary Service 8-40 p.m. (The Rev. E. J. G. Rogers, Bradford Diocesan Director of Education). Parade.
Thurs.	3	
Fri.	4	Fives: semi-final. Civics at 8 p.m. T. H. Somervell, Esq., F.R.C.S.
Sat.	5	VIth Form Reports.
S.	6	First Sunday in Lent. Preacher: The Rev. A. T. I. Boggis.
Mon.	7	Master of the week: Mr. MacDougall. Fives: final.
Tues.	8	Music Scholarship Examination. C.C.F. Field Day: Visit to School of Signals, Catterick.
Wed.	9	Voluntary Service 8-40 p.m.
Thurs.	10	C.C.F. Basic Test.
Fri.	11	
Sat.	12	4th Fortnight's Orders. Debating Society.
S.	13	Second Sunday in Lent. Holy Communion 8-15 and 11-40.
Mon.	14	Master of the week: Mr. Dawe.
Tues.	15	Reports to Form Masters. *All Sedberghian in.*

(handwritten marginalia: SEDBERGHIAN, Phoenix + Luptoni—)

(handwritten marginalia: LUPTONIAN IN)

Wed.	16	Voluntary Service 8-40 p.m. Parade.
Thurs.	17	Reports to Common Room. C.C.F. Army Proficiency Certificate.
Fri.	18	Last Day for Tradesmen's Orders.
Sat.	19	Reports to Housemasters 6 p.m. Subscription Concert 8 p.m.
S.	20	Third Sunday in Lent. Preacher: The Rev. T. A. Harman.
Mon.	21	Master of the week: Mr. Braham. Reports to Headmaster 8 p.m.
Tues.	22	The Wilson Run. Concert at 8 p.m.
Wed.	23	The Three Mile. Voluntary Service 8-40 p.m.
Thurs.	24	
Fri.	25	Annunciation of Blessed Virgin Mary. 5th Fortnight's Orders.
Sat.	26	Final Orders to Headmaster by 10 a.m.
S.	27	Fourth Sunday in Lent. Preacher: The Headmaster. Instrumental Competitions 8 p.m.
Mon.	28	Master of the week: Mr. Norwood. Singing Competitions 7-30 p.m. End of Term Service at 9-30 p.m.
Tues.	29	Term ends.

Next term begins on
Friday, 29th April and ends on Tuesday, 26th July.

My editorship of the *Sedberghian* and the school literary magazine, the *Phoenix*, are indicated in a list of some of the principal jobs in the school. These show the importance of getting the boys used to running small organizations and societies, including school teams and the library, which would prepare us for many professional tasks in later life.

THE LUPTONIAN

Vol. XIII   Spring, 1960   No. 1

Head of School:
C. J. Heber Percy.

Heads of Houses:
(SH) C. T. Lewis.
(E) F. G. Kenmir.
(L) I. C. Campbell.
(H) J. L. Bustard.
(P) J. T. Little
(W) C. J. Heber Percy.
(S) P. J. Mawby.

Football:
Capt.: A. H. Snodgrass.
Sec.: M. C. Hodgson.

Cricket:
Sec.: T. F. Greenshields.

Fives and Squash:
Sec.: T. F. Greenshields.

Swimming:
Sec.: D. A. B. Bagshaw.

Shooting:
Sec.: T. J. S. Bendle.

Tennis:
Sec.: A. I. Brodie-Smith

Senior Cadet:
C.S.M.:
D. A. B. Bagshaw.

"The Phoenix":
Editors:
C. J. Heber Percy.
A. D. J. Macfarlane
R. P. G. Moulding.

Library:
Librarian: A. J. Turnbull.
Curator: I. C. Campbell.
Classical Librarian:
M. T. Sykes.
Science Librarian:
A. J. M. Bone.
Mod. Language Librarian:

Art Librarian:
H. M. D. Brett.

Sedgwick Society:
Sec.: M. C. Hodgson.

"The Sedberghian":
Editors:
C. J. Heber Percy.
A. D. G. Macfarlane.
R. P. G. Moulding.
J. D. Whitman.

Treasurer:
G. H. Nelson.

Debating Society:
President:
T. F. Greenshields.
Secretary: F. G. Kenmir.

The Forum Society:
Chairman:
C. J. Heber Percy.
Secretary: M. T. Sykes.

44

FORMAL CLASSROOM EDUCATION

It is not easy to convey the intellectual side of school life, what happened in the classrooms and as we read and wrote through the years. The teachers at the school, like those at the Dragon, were largely the products of Oxford and Cambridge and hence were part of the long arch of an education from the age of eight which might lead me on to University. A slight preponderance for Cambridge (Cantab), may be a reflection of the founding of the school by a Cambridge scholar, Roger Lupton, and hence larger endowments and connections with that University, which continued with Henry Hart, the reviver of the school.

Headmaster:
G. M. C. THORNELY, M.A. (Cantab.)

Assistant Masters:
(34) L. R. TAYLOR, M.A. (Cantab.) (Second Master)
(36) C. R. WARD, M.A. (Cantab.)
(31) N. J. MAWBY, M.A., B.Sc. (Oxon.)
(17) K. C. BISHOP, M.B.E., M.A. (Cantab.)
 (7) O. M. FORSTER, M.A. (Cantab.)
(26) C. P. MARRIOTT, M.A. (Cantab.)
 (5) REV. A. T. I. BOGGIS, M.A. (Oxon.)
     A. E. HAMMER, M.A. (Cantab.)
(14) J. V. BEGLEY (Oxon.)
(25) W. T. GAIRDNER, M.A. (Oxon.),
                    Doct. de l' Univ. (Paris)
(12) L. P. MADGE, M. A. (Cantab.)
     E. P. E. LONG, M.A. (Liverpool),
                    Doct. de l' Univ. (Paris)
     A. L. MORGAN, D.S.C., M.A. (Oxon)
(21) D. B. ALBAN, M.A. (Cantab.)
 (9) H. H. MILLS, M.C., M.A., Ph.D. (Cantab.)
 (8) I. F. MacDOUGALL, M.A. (Cantab.)
 (6) R. W. W. DAWE, M.A. (Cantab.)
(11) P. J. BRAHAM, M.A. (Cantab.)
(20) D. P. NORWOOD, M.A. (Oxon.)
 (3) J. G. ROGERS, M.A. (Oxon.)
(10) REV. T. A. HARMAN, M.A. (Oxon.)
(39) C. J. BENNETT, B.A. (Cantab.)
     R. W. MOORE, B.A. (Cantab.)
 (1) E. W. T. KAYE, M.A. (Oxon.)
 (4) C. H. WILSON, B.A. (Oxon)
(19) J. A. TOWERS, M.A. (Cantab.)
 (2) N. P. C. P. MEADOWS, B.A. (Cantab.)
     D. B. HASSELL, M.A. (Oxon.)
     R. E. T. BIDDICK, B.A. (Cantab.)

The organization of the years and the classes is shown through the names of the masters and what they were responsible for. As with the Dragon, the main unit was the class, based on the central subject, for example history, languages or science, but alongside this were a parallel system of sets, so that we could move up or down in various subjects and were not constrained by our class position.

My progress was from IIIa, and 4a, in which I spent a year each. I and passed my exam at 16, G.C.S.E. (General Certificate of School Education or 'O' (Ordinary)) level in five subjects, English Language, Mathematics, Latin, French, History, but failing, like most in the school for some reason, my best subject, English Literature.

I then moved into the 'Classical Side' for my last three years, with a year in the Lower Sixth History (LCH), and two years (though I left before the final term having got a place at Oxford) in Clio, the History Sixth Form. I took my 'A' or 'Advanced Level' exams in the summer of my seventeenth year and got a distinction in English, a good pass in History and the General Paper, but failed the paper where we studied history through French and Latin texts. If I had been Oxbridge scholarship material I might, if my parents could afford it, have stayed on for an extra winter term for the scholarship exams.

CLASSICAL SIDE FORMS

	Latin	Greek	French	English
U6C	E.W.K.	E.W.K.	H.M.	J.G.R.

	History	English	French	Latin
CLIO	A.L.M.	D.B.A. H.H.M.	E.P.L.	C.H.W.

	French	German	English	Latin
ML6	W.T.G. H.H.M.	A.E.H.	J.V.B.	C.H.W.

	France	English	History	Geography
Gen. 6	D.B.H.	D.B.A.	A.L.M. C.P.M.	I.F.M.

	Latin	English	Mod. Hist.	Anc. Hist.
L6C	C.P.M.	J.V.B.	N.P.M.	C.P.M.
5aC	A.T.I.B.	N.P.M.	N.P.M.	
5bC	O.M.F.	O.M.F.	A.L.M.	French
L6H	O.M.F.	H.H.M. D.B.A.	J.G.R.	W.T.G.

MODERN SIDE FORMS

	Physics	Chemistry	English	French
U6Ma	R.W.M.	N.J.M.	J.V.B.	D.B.H.
U6Mb	L.R.T.	N.J.M.	D.B.A.	A.E.H.
Bio. 6	R.W.M.	C.J.B.	R.W.D.	D.B.A.
L6Ma	C.R.W.	C.J.B.	N.P.M.	
L6Mb	P.J.B.	N.J.M.	R.W.D.	
5aM	C.R.W.	L.P.M.	A.T.I.B.	K.C.B.
5bM	L.R.T.	C.J.B.	D.B.A.	W.T.G.

MIDDLE SCHOOL FORMS

	Latin	English	Physics	Chemistry
4a	C.H.W.	J.G.R.	C.R.W.	N.J.M.
4b	D.B.H.	T.A.H.	L.R.T.	L.P.M.
4c	Sets	R.W.D.	P.J.B.	R.W.M.
4d	Sets	N.P.M.	C.R.W.	C.J.B.

LOWER SCHOOL FORMS:

	Latin	English	History	Geography
IIIa	I.F.M.	R.W.D.	A.L.M.	R.W.D.
IIIb	C.H.W.	T.A.H.	J.G.R.	R.W.D.
IIa	N.P.M.	J.V.B.	J.V.B.	K.C.B.
IIb	R.W.D.	T.A.H.	R.W.D.	T.A.H

I had many good teachers, but the two who inspired me and shaped my future career as a university academic were my Clio history master, 'A.L.M', Andrew Morgan, and my English teacher, 'D.B.A.', David Alban, both of them outstanding teachers in different ways. Below are photographs of Andrew and David around the time they taught me.

The sets and their teachers show the other side of our teaching.

SET MASTERS

GREEK:		FRENCH:		MATHEMATICS:	
A C.P.M. .. 6		**Classical Side:**		U6M L.R.T.	
B E.W.K. .. 12		I W.T.G. ⎱ 11		D.P.N. ⎱ 33	
C C.H.W. .. 3		E.P.L. ⎰		B.A.T. ⎰	
GERMAN:		J H.H.M. .. 21			
V K.C.B. ..		K E.P.L. .. 22		**Upper School:**	
W A.E.H. .. 24				α J.A.T. .. 14	
X K.C.B. .. 24		**Middle School:**		β P.J.B. .. 6	
Y E.P.L. .. 24		1 D.B.H. .. 15			
Z D.B.H. .. 22		2a D.B.A. .. 20		γ D.P.N. .. 21	
ENGLISH:		2b H.H.M. .. 21		δ C.R.W. .. 16	
E O.M.F. .. 14		3a H.M. .. 20		ε R.W.M. .. 21	
		3b I.F.M. .. 16		ζ A.T.I.B. .. 22	
HISTORY:				η P.J.B. .. 18	
H N.P.M. ..		**Lower School:**			
LATIN:		4 W.T.G. .. 17			
Modern Side:		5 H.H.M. .. 17		**Middle School:**	
M C.H.W. ..		6 E.P.L. .. 19		θ J.A.T. .. 18	
N C.P.M. ..		7 A.E.H. . 12		κ D.P.N. .. 21	
				λ1 P.J.B. .. 24	
Middle School		**OPTIONS B:**		λ2 C.J.B. .. 15	
O A.T.I.B. ..		Gn K.C.B. ⎱ 11		μ O.M.F. .. 14	
P O.M.F. .. 19		R.T.B. ⎰ 8			
GEOGRAPHY:		Ru A.E.H. .. 15		**Lower School:**	
S I.F.M. .. 19		Ec J.G.R. ..		ρ A.T.I.B. 12	
T I.F.M. .. 11		Bi L.P.M. .. 14		σ R.W.M. .. 19	
		Mth J.A.T. ⎱		φ O.M.F. .. 24	
OPTIONS A:		C.R.W. ⎰ 15		ω T.A.H. .. 11	
Gt D.B.H. ⎱ 18		Art A.I. .. 20			
J.G.R. ⎰		Fr E.P.L. .. 15			
TCH. J.V.B. .. 20		Mus J.N.H.		**BIOLOGY:**	
Art A.I. .. 15		3 + 3 = 6		Bi 6 L.P.M 14	
Mus J.N.H. .. 2		K.A. ..		L6M L.P.M. 12	
K.A. ..		V.B. .. 7			
V.B. ..					

Clio was small and special, with only seventeen boys in the list for my last term.

CLIO.

Mr. Morgan

W	*C. J. HEBER PERCY 2m 3d (1)	Art
L	‡A. D. J. MACFARLANE 3m d	
H	M. Page 8m d	Ec
E	R. A. Collinge	Ec
L	††C. H. Vignoles 7m 2d	Gn
SH	H. McD. Young	Fr
W	**D. S. MACPHERSON**	Art
SH	C. T. LEWIS 2m	
L	G. H. Bland m	Art
W	†T. F. Greenshields 3m	
S	†A. J. Turnbull m	Bi
P	†J. Cameron d	Bi
S	**A. M. Stoddart**	Mths
E	†T. D. T. Hodson	Mus
L	D. S. Porter m	Mths
P	†**H. M. D. Brett** m	Mths
H	J. L. BUSTARD m	Ec

(17)   Average age 17.6.

(1) Evans Divinity Prize, 1958.
Weech History Prize, 1958.
VI Form Literature Prize, 1959.
Sterling English Verse Prize, 1959.
Craigmile Art Prize, 1959.
Heppenstall English Essay Prize, 1959.

The classroom was away from the rest of the school, next to Lupton House and across the road from the main place where we worked outside class, the school library housed within the original seventeenth century school building. The isolation from the rest of the physical structure of the school, combined with the way in which Morgan and Alban taught us, was enormously stimulating.

My time in Clio was the culmination of my schooling, but I had shown some ability from the start, largely because of the excellent education I had received at the Dragon. Having studied Macbeth as a Shakespeare play at the Dragon was no doubt behind my success in my second term in winning the Rankin Shakespeare Prize. The good teaching at the Dragon also allowed me to move up a class which later gave me the chance to compete for a university place.

85
105 *very good indeed.*

Sheet I   *Rankin Shakespeare 'Macbeth'*   A. Macfarlane 3

1. (a) It was said by Macbeth to Banquo's ghost
4   during the dinner scene.

(b) It was said by Banquo to Macbeth when they
4   were both travelling across the blasted heath to Forres
       after the battle, and they met the witches.

(c) It was said by Donaldbain to Malcom after
to 4   their father Duncan's body had been ~~disc~~ discovered
       and his sons were frightened of being murdered
       too.

(d) It was said by Macbeth to Macduff on
       the plateau in front of the castle when the
4   battle for the downfall of Macbeth was still
       raging.

(e) It was said by Macbeth when he ~~was~~ was
2   telling his wife about the sounds ^when he heard,
       just after the murder of Duncan.

(d) It was said by Macduff ~~of~~ to ~~R.~~ Malcom when
4   he hears the news that his wife and children
       have been
       ~~were~~ murdered by Macbeth.

22
24 v-g.

The teaching, as at the Dragon, consisted of frequent small lessons, usually three quarters of an hour or so, and then hurrying on to another subject. The topics we did in each class is indicated and the pattern is more or less repeated for the other four days until Saturday.

	MONDAY								TUESDAY				
	1	2	3	4	5	6	7	8	1	2	3	4	5
	9-10	10-0	11-0	11·45	12·30	4·15	5·0	5·45	9-10	10-0	11-0	11·45	12·30
U6 C	Cl	Cl		F	Cl	Cl CM 3	Cl		(Cl)	Cl 6			Cl 3
U6 Ma	M P 3	P M M		F	M P	M C (M) C	M C (M) C		(M)	E 6			C M M
U6 Mb	D AB	(M)		F 3	C	P	P	Art	(C) 3	P 6			M
Bi 6	Bi	E		P 3	D TH	C	C	or	C 3	Bi 6			P
CLIO	F	L		E	E	E HHM	H 3	Mus	E 6	H 3	PT b	Op. b	D AB
M L6	F HHM	Gn	PT a	F 3	(Gn)	CA JR	Gn		F F	Gn 3			E 6
Gen 6	E	D WG		Bg JR		Gy	E	E	Gy 3	(E)			MH 6
L6 C	LF WG 3	G G		Cl MH	Op. a	E	D	(E)	E	LF EL 3			G G 6
L6 H	L 3	D JR		E		F	H	H	H (3	F 3			E DA 3
L6 Ma	MC 3	P		D TH			M Bi	M Bi	(E)	C			P 3
L6 Mb	C	C		P 3				(E)		C 3			D TH
5a C	D	H 3		L		G G E	F	D	G G Lib			L	E 3
5b C	D AM	H 3	PT a	L	M			D AM	RD (3	M	PT b	L 3	E
5a M	D KB	C		L Gy		P 3	F	D CRW	P			L Gy	C (3
5b M	P 3	C				E	F	D TH	D CM	3		3	C (3
4a	D			C (3		L 3	D					C 3	
4b	D		F	C 3	PT g	G G	L	D	G G Art	F	M	P 3	PT h
4c	D PB			E		H Gy	D					P 3	
4d	P (3			C			D		(3	3		D TH	
IIIa	D				L (3	E 3	Gy	D	E (3	L			
IIIb	D		M	PT IIIb	L 3	Ws Dr	Ws Dr	D EK	M	H (3	L		F
IIa	D				L	Mus	E 3	D		L (3	Gy	PT IIb	
IIb	D				L 3	Gy 3	E	D	3	Gy	L (3		3

Currently many students around the world work for more than eight hours a day, six days a week, on class work and preparation. When I add up my own hours, I am amazed to find that on average we were probably only doing about five hours of class work a day for five and half days a week, and an hour or a little more of 'prep'. This gave us the time and energy to read round the subject, and to enjoy the many other forms of intellectual stimulus which I have described.

Another feature of the school, as at the Dragon, was the careful monitoring of our progress and the encouraging comments which our teachers sent in the termly reports to our parents. Important in these reports were also notes on our character and abilities outside the classroom, as in these two reports for my first and last terms.

Sedbergh School.

_____ SUMMER _____ Term, 19 59.   Name A.D.J. MACFARLANE.

House LUPTON   Age 17.9

Form.	Av. age.	No. of boys.	Starting Place.	Final Place.
CLIO	18.5	17	4	5

	Height.	Weight.	Girth.	
Commencing Term	56	9.5½	40½	
Ending Term	56½	9.6	39	

PRINCIPAL SUBJECTS. *History 9/15* Thoroughly conscientious work. Now that he has a body of knowledge behind him, he should be more adventurous in his expression of opinion. I expect him to take easily to more advanced work next year. *AJS*

English 9/15. Another very good term. His work is perceptive and scholarly in its thoroughness. *HMH* He has completed a year of sound work, and made great progress in every way. Most impressive to me quality of his reading; thorough, penetrating, and reliable. It's a pleasure to be in contact with one so responsive and so genuinely interested. *DBA*

SUBSIDIARY SUBJECTS.
1. General Japanese. He always makes a sensible and intelligent contribution. *LS*
2. LATIN. Another excellent term of highly industrious and intelligent work. *CHW*
3. Divinity. Very good progress. Original thought, and thoroughly sound. *T.A.H.*
4. French. Good thorough work on set books; accents rather uncertain at times. *PR*

N.B Music Satisfactory. *VB.*

MUSIC (Guitar) Good work *BP*   ART

HOUSEMASTER Continued excellent progress. I look forward to having him as a prefect next term and I'm sure he will do the job as well as he does everything else he undertakes. *MM*

HEADMASTER He is developing most promisingly. *(initials)*

Next term begins on SEPTEMBER 18TH 19 59.
All boys must return on that day, unless they have leave of absence from the Headmaster.
Parents can obtain this leave through the Housemaster, to whom the earliest possible inform-

The encouragement and careful attention to our work, watching over our shoulders to see how we moved on and quite gently correcting and advising, is shown in the numerous essays I have kept. Just one example from Andrew Morgan, commenting on my first essay when I joined Clio (on the Renaissance), and from David Alban in my last year (on Jane Austen), shows the care and encouragement we were given. Our work was not only approaching University level, but the supervision methods were a foretaste of what I tried to practice through my forty years as an academic at Cambridge University.

that sort of humour?

be complete. Lastly of course she is the
suitable object from which Jane Austen can
draw her humour, a humour nevertheless which
is kind and gentle. The authoress's views on this
matter and Lady Russell's essential qualities
are shown in the following passage." There is
a quickness of perception in some, ···· a natural
penetration in short, ···· Lady Russell had been
less gifted in this than her young friend. But
she was a very good woman, and if her second
object was to be sensible and well-judging,
her first was to see Anne happy. She loved
Anne better than she loved her own abilities;··"

———— ‖ ————

A very good piece of work, revealing close
and careful study of the text. You should
have made rather more of the excellent point
you make at the bottom of the second page,
because this is one of Jane Austen's principal methods
of conveying comedy in her characterisation.
Also, try to you must always be alive to the
spirit of laughing irony which pervades the whole thing

145

SEVEN

Oxford Undergraduate
1960 – 1963

A GAIN FOLLOWING MY uncle Robert, I went from Worcester to Worcester College, Oxford in October 1960 to read history. By chance I discovered that it was arguably the most beautiful small College, and my two main history teachers were among the best in the University. As well as finding increasing delight in my work, I had my first two serious love affairs over these three years and made deep friendships with several of my year group.

It was all a magical release from the severities of the northern boy's school and I loved all of my time there, even if there were conflicts over sex, religion and moments of self-doubt. I finished on the borderline of obtaining a first class degree in history.

The original medieval College to which I went was called Gloucester Hall and had been set up as a training centre for the Benedictine religious order in the south of England. The earlier shape, and the medieval terrace which still survives gave the College a homely feel. To the old buildings, there had been added an eighteenth century library and dining hall, and a long terrace where I used to go for my supervisions in the first year.

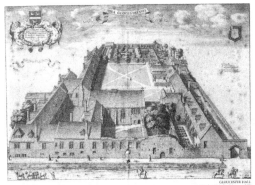

GLOUCESTER HALL
after a drawing by David Loggan c 1675

Oxford, Worcester College Quadrangle. (Founded A. D. 1714).

One of the two entrances to the garden was through a tunnel under my teacher's garden, supposedly the inspiration for Alice's descent into Wonderland, and I certainly felt an enchantment whenever I went through it, as I still do when I return many decades later.

Soon you reached a lake, which was was the backdrop to magical plays and concerts, and I walked past the old bent tree almost every day in earnest conversation with my friends.

I spent the first year in College accomodation next to the
main theatre in Oxford, three minutes from the College. Here
I remember the delights of having a large room of my own,
one stage beyond the prefect's study at Sedbergh, a place I
could entertain in (I still remember buying tea cups from Wools-
worths store and the pride with which I gave my first tea party).
I described the room in my first letter home.

~~to dinner~~ in Hertford.

After a fairly hectic journey over here I arrived at about 1.0 at Oxford station - and waited about ¾ of an hour for a taxi! When the "scout" (a 17ᵗʰ Smith - a *very* nice and helpful person) showed me my room she said it was the best in the hostel - and I think she was right. The hostel itself is between the "theatre" and the Randolph Hotel - about 3 minutes walk (at the far end of the street) from Worcester.

My room is quite large - ~~a bit~~ a bit smaller than the drawing room but slightly higher-ceilinged. It has two built in clothes cupboards ~~etc~~ I enclose a drawing which will save much description.

dinner table (covered by my mexican rug) The

Clothes & tea-set built-in cupboard gas stove yes it is table with gramaphon

it route over the roof into the 'can park for getting in cars at right! large desk with 8 drawers washbasin & underneath gas-meter (both enclosed)

bed (very comfortable). door.

- I expect you are none the wiser - but it is a lovely room - with a nice carpet - a very comfortable armchair - and you can

In the second year we lived in College. I chose to live in what I now discover was the very oldest part of the College, above what had been the medieval kitchen (the chimney is clearly visible, with my window half way up on the right). It was here that I became really involved with history, learnt to type and file my materials, and moved up and beyond the level I had reached in Sedbergh. I 'came out' really in this year, after a first year of preliminary exploration.

The College was a community. We not only slept and studied there but also ate together in the eighteenth century hall, observing the many strange small rituals of drinking and toasting our friends. This medieval religious communal eating was a continuation of what I had first encountered at the Dragon, and was to enjoy for many decades in my final destination in Cambridge. It forced you to sit next to people from all kinds of subjects, and you were obliged to talk to them rather than friends in your own discipline. There was a rule that you must not talk 'shop', that is about your own subject to a friend in the same field, on pain of being 'sconced' (that is forced to buy beer for all the surrounding people who overheard you). Along with the communal Common Room, which was next to my second year bedroom, this is the core of the interdisciplinary nature of Oxbridge life.

It was a community that was changing very rapidly in my time. Ten years earlier (when the painting below was done), the clothing, gestures, sports, all indicate a public school male world, often with older young men who had done two years of army training (National Service).

By 1960 when I arrived (I am third from the left in the front row in this photograph in 1961) the undergraduates were younger and more informally dressed, a reasonable number (for example half of my closest friends) were from grammar rather than public schools, and we were starting to show the influence of the huge cultural changes ('Angry Young Men', Elvis and soon the Beatles) of the late 1950's and early 1960's. It was the cusp of a revolution and full of energy and idealism.

It was in these three years that I turned from a late teenager, through my twenty-first birthday, to the young man who went out into the world and worked at my first real job in a Youth Hostel in the Lake District.

All of this was an amazing and enriching experience. But it came at a cost, not merely emotional, psychological and intellectual, but in economic terms. I had been awarded a Lancashire County Council grant which paid for most of my basic costs, so, with the help of my parents for some pocket money, I did not need to work in the holidays, nor did I run up a debt. I managed my own bank account and lived modestly, but reasonably. The costs are laid out on the termly schedule of payments of 'battels' as they were called. In this, my first term, I spent only a modest amount on 'drinks', which could be purchased at meals or in the small 'buttery' or bar near the hall. I belonged to various clubs and paid tuition fees and laundry and fuel.

WORCESTER COLLEGE, OXFORD

Battels for Michaelmas Term, 1960

A.D.J. Macfarlane, Esq.,
Field Head,
Outgate,
Nr. Ambleside, Lancs.

	£	s.	d.
Inclusive charge for Board and Lodging	59.	4.	O.
Meals in Hall			
Guests Meals			
Guests Accommodation			
Milk, Tea, Coffee and Stores ...			
Drinks		. 7	9
Coupons			
Gratuities	2.	0.	0
Laundry	1.	9.	11
Fuel		. 2.	6
Gate Fines			
Postage and Messenger		.	2
J.C.R. Art Fund			
Damage			
Library—Book Fines			
Junior Common Room		15.	0
College Clubs	3.	5.	0
University and College Dues ...	28.	4.	0
	95	.8	.4
Tuition Fee	35.	0.	0
Key Deposits			
B.U. Provident Association	1.	1.	0
Oxford Society			
Debtor Balance brought forward ...			
Prepayment for H.T. 1961	25.	0.	0
	146	.9	.4

Credit:	£	s.	d.
Prepayment for M.T. 1960...	25.	0.	0
Credit Balance of last account			
Scholarship			
Exhibition			
Ministry of Education ...			
Local Authority	58.	4.	0
Cash			
		83 .4 .0	
Balance Due to the College	£	63 .5 .4	

The College meets for next term on Friday, 13th January, 1961 and these battels must be paid before that date.

The whole of this form, with the appended slip completed, should be forwarded with your remittance for the exact amount to National Provincial Bank Limited, 32, Cornmarket Street, Oxford. Cheques should be made payable to Worcester College, Oxford.

At Sedbergh and at home in the Lake District, the amount of 'culture', and even the opportunities to join clubs and associations, was fairly limited. It was extraordinary to arrive at Oxford, with four good cinemas, two excellent theatres (one next door), numerous concert halls, endless clubs and groups of people wanting to share some hobby or passion. It is difficult to convey this briefly, but let me start with what was publicly advertized in the Oxford magazine 'Vade Mecum' as available for the first four days after I arrived in 1960. Here we have films, sermons, clubs of various kinds, religious groups, talks, operas and the theatre.

---

buy OXFORD OPINION

ALL TIMES ARE P.M. UNLESS OTHERWISE STATED

FIRST WEEK DIARY

Scala Cinema : Vittorio de Sica and Sophia Loren in "L'oro di Napoli" and "The Lost Continent."
Ritz Cinema : "A French Mistress."
Super Cinema : "Green Mare's Nest" and "Wages of Fear."
Regal Cinema : "The Young have no time" and "More Deadly than the Male."

SUNDAY, 9th OCTOBER
OI CCU : Rev. J. A. Motyer, Freshmen's Sermon. Wesley Memorial Church, 8.30.
Friends' Society : Harold Loukes' "Lost Causes and Screaming Tyres." 43 St. Giles, 12.45.

MONDAY, 10th OCTOBER
Humanist Group : Social, Union Cellars, 8.15.
Labour Club : Open Meeting. Ralph Samuel "Can Socialism Survive?" Ruskin, 4.30.
Badminton Club : Trials. Manor Road Court.

TUESDAY, 11th OCTOBER
SCM : Canon T. R. Milford (Master of the Temple) "Why Christianity?" Wesley Mem. Church, 8.15.
OU Cross Country : University Trials.
Humanist Group : F. A. Ridley (Pres. Nat. Secular Soc.) "On Rome." Taylor Institute, 8.15.
Badminton Club : Trials. Manor Road Club.

WEDNESDAY, 12th OCTOBER
Cosmos : Sir William Hayter "Soviet Foreign Policy." Rhodes House, 8.15.
Medical Society : Prof. Sir Alistair Hardy "Did Man have a more Aquatic Past?" Radcliffe Infirmary, 8.15.
CND : Social. Union Cellars. 8.15.
French Club : "Vive! Monsieur Blaireau." School of Botany, South Parks Road, 8.
Crime—A Challenge : Open Meeting. Prof. Radzinowicz "The Study of Criminology." Rhodes House, 8.15.
Opera Club : "Il Seraglio." Holywell Music Room, 8.
E.T.C. : Dame Peggy Ashcroft. 8.15.

18

The film experience was particularly rich, for instance here is the programme for just one cinema – the Scala or 'Arts' cinema, for one term. I went to a number of extraordinary films, particularly French, Japanese and new wave, during my three years.

I also went to wonderful plays and musical performances of all kinds in College gardens and in the Oxford Playhouse. Particularly memorable was my first sudden realization of how wonderful Mozart was in a concert and set of readings, accompanied by wine, under the theme 'Murder and Mozart'. I also particularly remember the three plays put on in the beautiful Worcester gardens, including 'Penny for a Song', and 'Measure for Measure' in which I rather shakily sang to my guitar 'Take oh take those lips away…'

Every College had musical performances, and there were numerous choirs and orchestras, as well as many distinguished visiting
singers and players.

BALLIOL COLLEGE MUSICAL SOCIETY

1260TH CONCERT: SUNDAY, OCTOBER 22ND, 1961
At **9.0** p.m. (Doors open at 8.45 p.m.)

QUARTET IN F MINOR, Op. 20, No. 5 - *Haydn* (1732–1809)
    Allegro moderato
    Minuetto
    Adagio
    Fuga a due soggetti

QUARTET No. 6 - - - - *Villa-Lobos* (1887–1959)
    Poco animato
    Allegretto
    Andante quasi adagio
    Allegro vivace

QUARTET IN A MINOR, Op. 51, No. 2 - *Brahms* (1833–97)
    Allegro non troppo
    Andante moderato
    Quasi minuetto, moderato
    Allegro non assai

WANG STRING QUARTET

Alfredo Wang (*Violin*)   Gordon Mutter (*Viola*)
Stanley Popperwell (*Violin*)   George Isaac (*Cello*)

NEXT CONCERT: Sunday, November 5th, at 9.0 p.m. Recital by
Bruno Hoffmann (*Glass Harp*).

The recitals and performances covered the whole spectrum, including poetry and jazz. And I joined the local folk and blues singing club, which met at a local pub and where again there were some amazing performers, whose work I had only heard on records or radio.

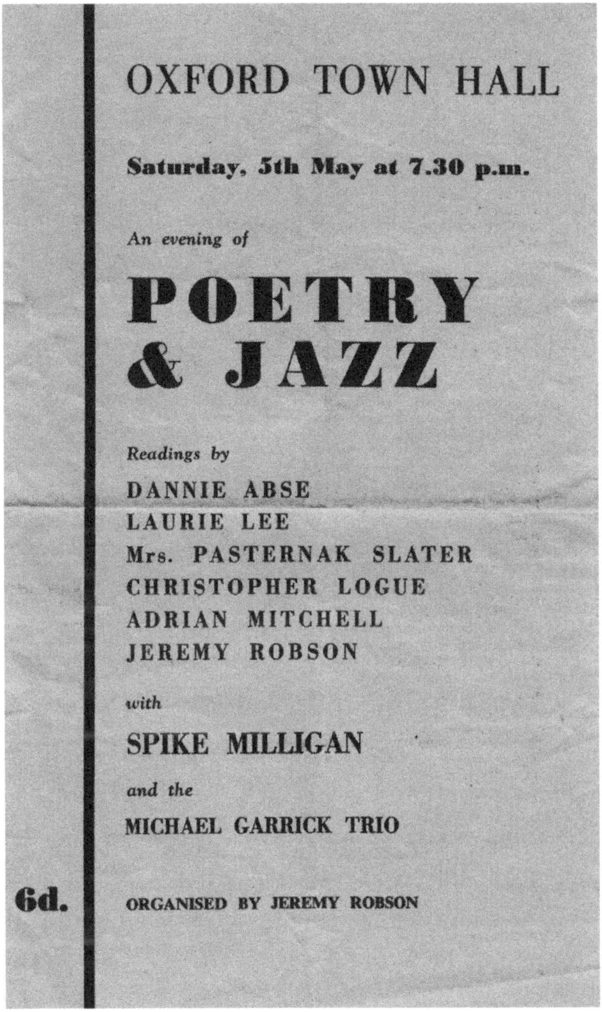

OXFORD TOWN HALL

Saturday, 5th May at 7.30 p.m.

An *evening* of

POETRY
& JAZZ

Readings *by*

DANNIE ABSE
LAURIE LEE
Mrs. PASTERNAK SLATER
CHRISTOPHER LOGUE
ADRIAN MITCHELL
JEREMY ROBSON

with

SPIKE MILLIGAN

and the

MICHAEL GARRICK TRIO

6d.   ORGANISED BY JEREMY ROBSON

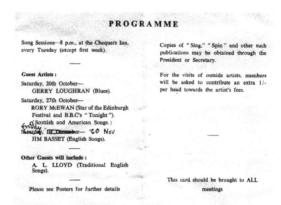

The numerous activities are again shown briefly in what was happening in just one small College, Worcester, in my second week, which I have annotated with one or two extra engagements.

Before turning to further activities, it is worth pausing on a central feature of all this, which was friendship and collegiality. My earlier years, especially the last two at boarding school, had taught me the pleasure of real friendships, but it was at university that this developed fastest. There were many male friends, from all backgrounds, with whom I went on picnics, played games, and went on a walking tour to the Outer Hebrides in my second year.

I also went with some of my College friends to spend time with young men who were in a Borstal, or young person's prison. We camped with them in the Yorkshire moors and then visited their prison. (I am washing up in the bottom row).

With these friends I also played formal games, joining the Worcester football team (overleaf, top right) for a fairly packed schedule of games.

Date		Opponents			Ground	Result

FIRST XI

Date		Opponents			Ground	Result
JANUARY						
Monday	22	St. Peter's	...	...	Home	
Saturday	27	Emmanuel, Cambridge		...	Away	
Monday	29	Balliol	...	...	Away	
FEBRUARY						
Thursday	1	Corpus Christi	...	...	Away	
Monday	5	Queen's	...	...	Away	
Saturday	10	Old Bradfieldians	...	...	Home	
Monday	12	Magdalen	...	...	Away	
Saturday	17	Salesian College	...	...	Home	
Monday	19	St. Catherine's	...	...	Away	
Thursday	22	Wadham	...	...	Home	
Monday	26	City Police	...	...	Home	
MARCH						
Thursday	1	Pembroke	...	...	Home	
Monday	5	St. Edmund Hall	...	...	Away	
Thursday	8	Merton	...	...	Away	
Saturday	10	New College	...	...	Away	
Tuesday	13	Brasenose	...	...	Home	

SECOND XI

Date		Opponents			Ground	Result
JANUARY						
Tuesday	23	Wycliffe Hall	...	...	Away	
Tuesday	30	Balliol	...	...	Home	
FEBRUARY						
Tuesday	6	St. Peter's	...	...	Home	
Tuesday	13	Pembroke	...	...	Away	
Tuesday	20	Ruskin College	...	...	Home	
Tuesday	27	St. Catherine's	...	...	Away	
MARCH						
Thursday	8	Brasenose	...	...	Away	
Monday	12	Queen's	...	...	Away	

By careful time managing, which became an obsession, I was able to fit in many other clubs, some philanthropic, some political (as with the Union Society whose debates for one term are listed). I was particularly idealistic at this stage and worked at the newly founded OXFAM (Oxford Committee for Famine Relief), and visited hospitals for sick children. I was also a representative for a while of the United Nations club – Cosmos – and social secretary for the Union Society.

1st Debate. 19th October.

"That this House has no confidence in Her Majesty's Government."

MR. MICHAEL STEWART, M.P.   MR. DENZIL FREETH, M.P.

2nd Debate. 26th October.

"That in the opinion of this House this country should unilaterally renounce any policy based on Nuclear Weapons."

MR. EMRYS HUGHES, M.P.   MR. CONSTANTINE FITZGIBBON.

3rd Debate. 2nd November.

"That this House deplores the Americanization of British culture."

MR. CHRISTOPHER HOLLIS.   HON. WILLIAM DOUGLAS-HOME.

4th Debate. 9th November.

"That this House welcomes the Government's decision to seek entry to the European Economic Community."

MR. ANTHONY GREENWOOD, M.P. SIR EDWARD BOYLE, BT., M.P.

Speakers' Classes will be held on Wednesdays at 2.0 p.m. during 2nd—5th weeks inclusive of term.

5th Debate. 16th November.

"That in the opinion of this House the reunification of Germany should not be the object of Western policy."

MR. SEFTON DELMER, O.B.E. BARON RÜDIGER VON PACHELBEL.

6th Debate. 23rd November.

"That in the opinion of this House the machinery of Mass Publicity should be demolished."

MR. JOHN WAIN   MR. FRANCIS WILLIAMS, C.B.E.

7th Debate. 30th November.   PRESIDENTIAL.

"That in the opinion of this House moderation is not a reliable principle for politics."

MR. R. H. S. CROSSMAN, O.B.E., M.P.

8th Debate. 7th December.   FAREWELL.

"That this House prefers Saturday night to Sunday morning."

There will also be an additional Freshmen's Debate on Tuesday, November 21st.

COSMOS

OFFICERS — MICHAELMAS TERM 1961

Patrons

MADAM VIJAYA LAKSHMI PANDIT
DR. RALPH BUNCHE
LORD BEVERIDGE, K.C.B.
MR. DAVID OWEN

Senior Members

SIR WILLIAM HAYTER, K.C.M.G. (New College)
MR. L. J. COHEN, M.A. (Queen's)
DR. Z. A. PELCZYNSKI (Pembroke)

President
JOHN GELLING (Keble)

Vice-President
MIKE DAVIS (Exeter)

SECRETARY: ROBERT SPEED (Worcester)
TREASURER: MALCOLM MULLINS (S.E.H.)
SOCIAL SECRETARY: DAVID ATWILL (University)
Committee:
Organising Secretary: PETER MORLEY (Ch.Ch.)
Asst. Organising Secretary: RICHARD SMETHURST (Worcester)
Assistant Secretary: CHRISTOPHER McCANN (Lincoln)
War on Want Secretary: SARAH GRETTON (L.M.H.)
Travel Department: MICHAEL SANDFORD (Lincoln)
Work Camps, Careers
Orient-Occident
Committee:
Chairman: ANANT KIRPAL (Worcester)
Secretary: STEPHEN LINSTEAD (C.C.C.)
Delegate WUS, GMG,
JACARI: TIM BULLICK (Worcester)
Dinners Secretary: CHRIS EAMES (Merton)
Delegate City UNA,
OXFMENT: CHRIS JERVIS (Exeter)
Delegate Refugee
Committee: SINNYSAY VILAY (Worcester)
Ex-President COSMOS,
Treasurer UNSA: MARC LEE (Exeter)
Ex-President UNSA,
Publicity Secretary UNSA: HUGH WILCOX (SEH)

SOCIAL PROGRAMME — IKHWAN ES SAFA

Friday, 27th October at 8.15 p.m.   Union Cellars
COSMOS SOCIAL
Dancing to the Swing Sextet.

Tuesday, 31st October at 8.15 p.m. Worcester Memorial Room
INTERNATIONAL AT HOME
Our traditional Wine and Cheese party. All students from abroad are invited: other members of COSMOS should apply to the Social Secretary.

Sunday, 12th November at 8.15 p.m.   Union Cellars
COSMOS CHARITY SOCIAL
Dancing to the Swing Sextet.

The attention of COSMOS members is drawn to the following:

Tuesday, 24th October   United Nations Day

Saturday, 4th November at 2.30 p.m.   S.E.H. 3.20
Donald Tweddle—"The Freedom from Hunger Campaign"
(For members of the South Midland U.N. Student Associations visiting Oxford, and COSMOS.)

Sunday, 5th–12th November   U.N. Refugee Week

Wednesday, 8th November   Rhodes House
Peter Casson
(British Representative of the U.N. High Commissioner for Refugees.)

"After WRY—Refugees and World Want"
(Joint meeting with OUCA, OU Labour Club, OU Liberal Club, WUS, SCM, Newman Soc., OU Anglican Fellowship and COSMOS.)

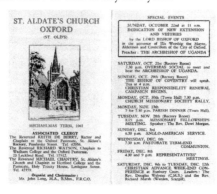

COMPLIMENTARY TICKET.

Alan Macfarlane

FREEDOM FROM HUNGER LECTURES

Wesley Memorial Hall, New Inn Hall Street, at 8 p.m.

1st May	"World Food and Population"	Thomas Balogh, M.A., Lecturer in Economics, Balliol College.
8th May	"Nutrition and Health"	Dr. H.M.Sinclair, B.Sc., D.M., Reader in Human Nutrition, Magdalen College.
15th May	"Community Development"	W.H.Beckett, M.A., Demon-strator and Lecturer in Agric-ultural Economics, Balliol College.
22nd May	"The Campaign in the United Kingdom"	D.Tweddle, General Secretary, U.K. Committee Freedom from Hunger.

These lectures are being arranged by the United Nations Association in co-operation with the Oxford Committee for Famine Relief. The Freedom from Hunger Campaign has a paramount importance in creating the climate of public opinion that will make possible the economic development of the underdeveloped countries. If hunger and poverty are ever to be cleared from the face of this earth both knowledge and action must be harnessed into constructive channels.

You are invited to these special meetings with the hope that you will bring with you as many interested friends as possible.

The Borstal camp and some of the other activities were inspired by religion, and this was in some ways my most religious phase. I immediately started to attend St Aldate's, an evangelical church, and went weekly to the Worcester College chapel, where I would make confession and became a friend of the Chaplain. I also went again to the boy's religious camp I had attended as a child and adolescent, run by Oxford and Cambridge figures. Much of my casual writing of the time, as well as letters to parents and girl-friends, was concerned with an attempt to retain my Christian belief in the face of increasing doubt – which finally overcame me more or less in my last year.

I was still close to my family, and was visited by my sisters several times. I spent wonderful holidays in our Lake District home and had another circle of friends there. I wrote weekly to my parents, who were away in India for almost all of my undergraduate years, and received long letters from my mother almost every week. We started to discuss intellectual matters and I tried to share my happiness and ideas I was encountering within and without the formal history syllabus.

Yet I was also making my first steps to the new type of relationship which would finally establish me as an adult away from my family, namely serious romantic attachments. It was this which made Oxford not only even more beautiful than it seemed on the surface, but form the strongest memories of

what seemed to be an extaordinary change in my life. I had two
serious and very idealistic love affairs during my time, which
included going out on punts, going to parties and many long
and intense discussions. Through these I learnt a great deal
about myself and prepared myself for my final breaking away
from my family through marriage.

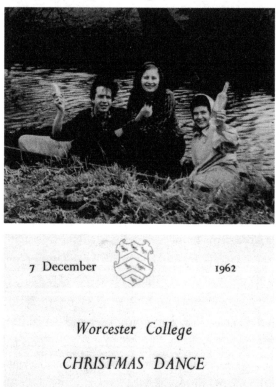

7 December   1962

Worcester College

CHRISTMAS DANCE

9.00 p.m.   *Double Ticket*

FORMAL HISTORY TEACHING

As with the Dragon and Sedbergh, I have left the formal work on intellectual matters, the reading of history for three years in order to become a Bachelor and then Master of Arts, to the end. It was the centre of my experience, for I took it very seriously, worked hard and enjoyed it. But it cannot be understood except in the previous context of a total emotional and social experience of widening horizons. I matured intellectually alongside psychological changes, so that by the end of the three years I was no longer a sixth form historian, but ready, if necessary, to become a teacher, civil servant, trainee lawyer or doctor.

It is only now that I realize how fortunate I was in my choice of subject, university and college. Oxford was at that time the leading school of history in the world and I was lectured by some of the greatest British historians. Half of the lecture list for one term gives an idea of the formal lectures we could attend, though it was customary only to go to three or four series a week (those I attended are marked overleaf), almost all held in College lecture rooms or dining halls.

FACULTY OF MODERN HISTORY

Lecture List for Trinity Term 1961

Subject	Lecturer	Time	Place	Course begins
BRITISH HISTORY				
The Celtic Background of Early Anglo-Saxon History (one lecture)	Mrs. N. K. Chadwick (O'Donnell Lecturer in Celtic Studies)	F. 5 (19 May)	Schools	
Justice in Medieval England	Miss N. D. Hurnard	T. Th. 11	"	
The Government of England 1066–1307	Mr. H. E. Bell	W. 11	New College	
Stephen's Reign (1135–54)	Mr. R. H. C. Davis	F. 10	Merton	
The English Church after the Conquest	Mrs. S. M. Wood	W. 12	Schools	
The English Church in the Thirteenth Century	Mr. W. A. Pantin	S.10	"	
Towns, Trade, and Population in the Later Middle Ages	Miss B. Harvey	M. 10	"	
The Hundred Years War and English Society	Mr. K. B. McFarlane	W. 11	Magdalen	
The English Church in the Fifteenth Century	Dr. V. H. H. Green	F. 10	Lincoln	
The Coming of the English Revolution 1529–1641	Mr. L. Stone	W. F. 10	Wadham	
The Reign of Charles II	Mr. P. G. M. Dickson	F. 12	St. Catherine's	
India 1707–1907 (Selected Topics)	Mr. C. C. Davies	T. 10	Indian Institute	
The Origins of Methodism	Dr. V. H. H. Green	F. 12	Lincoln	
Religion and Society in Nineteenth-century England	Mrs. J. M. Hart	T. 12	Schools	
The House of Lords in the Nineteenth Century	Mrs. C. R. Dick	M. 12	"	
British Foreign Policy 1815–1914	Mr. A. E. Campbell	Th. 12	Keble	
British Social and Economic History from 1815 (first four weeks)	Mr. D. T. Healey	F. 11	Barnett House	
The British Conservative Party 1846–1914	Mr. A. E. Firth	W. 11	University	
Imperial Defence as a Factor in the Evolution of the Commonwealth 1830–1914	Mr. D. K. Fieldhouse	W. 10	Rhodes House	
Joseph Chamberlain: a Reappraisal	Mr. M. C. Hurst	Th. 10	St. John's	
British Constitutional History 1914–1953 (Le May Documents) (About four lectures to conclude)	Professor Beloff	Th. 10	All Souls	
The Evolution of the Commonwealth 1919–1961 (Keith, &c.)	Dr. A. F. Madden	M. 10	Rhodes House	
**GENERAL HISTORY				
The Councils of Ephesus and Chalcedon (I, I)	Mr. A. G. Mathew	M. 11	Blackfriars	
Religion and Society in the Age of St. Augustine (I, I)	Mr. P. R. L. Brown	T. 11	All Souls	
Introduction to the Corpus Iuris Canonici (II, III, II, III, IV)	Mr. E. W. Kemp	S. 10	Exeter	
Europe in the Tenth Century (II, III, II, III, IV)	Mr. A. D. M. Cox	Th. 11	University	
Germany 919–1056: Society, Economy, and Culture (III, III, IV)	Mr. K. J. Leyser, X.	Th. 12	Magdalen	
The Mediterranean World in the Twelfth Century in the Travels of Benjamin of Tudela (III, IV, V)	Dr. Roth	F. 11	History Faculty Library	
The Fourteenth Century Renaissance (IV, V, VI)	Mr. A. G. Mathew	T. 11	Balliol	
The Economic Development of Western Europe in the Later Middle Ages (IV, V, V, VI, VII) (two lectures to conclude)	Mr. P. S. Lewis	M. Th. 11	All Souls	
European History in the Fifteenth Century (IV, V, VI, VII)	Mr. C. A. J. Armstrong	W. 10	Hertford	
The Papacy in the Fifteenth Century (IV, V, VI, VII)	Miss M. E. Reeves	T. 10	Schools	
Cusanus (four lectures) (IV, V, VI, VII)	Professor Jacob	T. 11	All Souls	
Renaissance Warfare: Social and Technical Aspects (seminar) (V, VI, VI, VII, VIII)	Mr. J. R. Hale	F. 5	Jesus	
Problems in Spanish History (Fifteenth and Early Sixteenth Centuries) (IV, V, VI, VII, VIII)	Dr. J. R. L. Highfield	Th. 12	Merton	
Cujus Regio, ejus religio 1555–1697 (VI, VIII, IX, X)	Dr. J. W. Stoye	Th. 10	Schools	
Maritime Aspects 1559–1648 (VI, VIII, IX)	Mr. E. H. F. Smith	F. 10	St. Peter's Hall	
European Peace Treaties 1559–1715 (VI, VIII, IX, X)	Professor Wernham	M. 12	Schools	
General Problems in European History in the First Half of the Seventeenth Century (VI, VIII, IX)	Mr. J. P. Cooper	M. 11	Trinity	
The Russian Empire and the West in the Eighteenth Century (VI, VII, IX, X, XI)	Dr. N. Zernov	Th. 10	Keble	
France and Europe 1789–1814 (VII, VIII, XI. XII)	Mr. C. H. Stuart	M. W. 10	Christ Church	

My second good fortune was in my teachers at Worcester. The College had two of the best tutors, James Campbell for Anglo-Saxon and medieval history, and Harry Pitt for the eighteenth and nineteenth centuries.

The degree course was mainly concerned with the history of England between the end of the Roman occupation of Britain and 1914. There were also a few extra themes and topics. In the first term we prepared for the only formal university written exams we would take before our Final exams at the end of three years. These were called 'Prelims' and consisted of the study of historiography as represented by Edward Gibbon, Thomas Babington Macaulay, Alexis de Tocqueville and the

Venerable Bede. There were also Latin and French tests based on the latter two authors. Like several of my friends I failed a paper, the Latin unseen, but fortunately managed to pass on the retake. James Campbell tells me that if I had failed again I would probably have been sent down (expelled) from Oxford.

In our third and fourth term we chose a period of European history and I studied later medieval and the early modern period. In Spring and Summer terms of 1962 I studied political theory, basically Aristotle, Hobbes and Rousseau, with some J.S. Mill and Marx at the end.

In the last academic year we chose a special subject which was to introduce us to the use of original sources and I studied the Interregnum of Oliver Cromwell. We also chose a special theme, in my case Tudor and Stuart economic history. In the spring term of our last year we did some wider general reading under the guidance of Harry Pitt and then some revision tutorials with both Harry and James in our last term, accompanied on warm summer days with a pint of beer.

There were several different ways in which we learnt. One was through writing a long essay roughly every week which we would take to an hour-long tutorial where, usually paired with another student, we would either read it out or listen to the other essay and the comments of our tutor. These tutorials were the really special part of my Oxford education. I had experienced them in a simpler form at Sedbergh, but my teachers were now expecting higher level work and the grilling was more intense.

I have kept all my essays, but will only give one example – the first page of a four page essay I wrote for my special subject on economic history in my penultimate term. This is hand-written, though I started to type my essays towards the end.

Essay 2.   12/7/63.

With what aims and what success did governments attempt to control industry during the sixteenth and seventeenth centuries?

Roughly speaking, though generalisation is always dangerous in economic history a government would have one or a mixture more of the following aims in its policy towards industry. It would seek financial benefits, encouraging production as a means to increasing trade and hence customs or more indirectly by issuing rewarding licences and monopolies. Allied to this was a desire to retain a favourable balance of trade, to stimulate home manufacture, especially of expensive luxury goods which were steadily imported, and thus to increase national wealth. Such a theory lies behind the words of the Knight in the 'Commonweal of the Realm (1549) when he warns "that imports should be lessened by encouraging "cappers, glovers, paper makers, goldsmiths, blacksmiths of all sorts, needle makers, pinners" and so on to produce and export "for we must always take heed that we buy no more of strangers than we sell them" – for if we do, he argues, we impoverish ourselves and enrich them. The above is the purely economic aspect of industry and the application of government pressure in this sphere can be found in regulation of the Exchange and coinage, in the issuing of patents, for instance that for salt to Thomas Wilkes in 1586, or for soap in 1623 to Roger Jones and Andrew Palmer. Let us examine for a moment the success of the government in achieving this aim in just two of its projects – salt and alum workings.

The attempts of the English monarchs to participate in the manufacture of salt began in Elizabeth's; for, as Nef shows, the salt output went up by x 5 between 1540–1640. Remembering the French gabelle English statesmen made plans for claiming land between low and high tide as the property of the state. Plans were made in 1563 by [HUGHES & STILES] & Mon Cecil and others to bring in foreign workmen and advances (salt pans) capital (of 'Mines Royal') for starting an enterprise with branches at Southampton. Dover & along the coasts of Essex & Norfolk. By letters patent of 1564 the crown tried to establish a notional monopoly of the sale of salt from sea water. Nothing came of the project. The plant was set up. Contracts were entered into, but the iron pans of W'd were rusting away unused 5 yrs after they had been installed. Thus the claim of the crown in regalian right in salt marches along the coasts fared little better in the common

Another teaching method was particularly important in the first term and in the special subjects – Cromwell and economic history – where there were set texts. These were the 'gobbets'. These consisted of short essays of less than a page each commenting on some quotations from our chosen authors. We were asked to set the passages in their proper context and explain the wider significance of the quoted extract. Again this was something I had been introduced to in my last two years at Sedbergh but it was now more stringently marked. Here again is one example.

In preparation for the essays and gobbets we were set a good deal of reading to do both before each essay and in the fairly long vacations (over half the year) and were sometimes required to do an essay or two as well out of term. We were tested on this reading, as well as our previous term's work at the start of each new term in what were called 'Collections'. These were done on the first Friday and Saturday morning of the term, and consisted of two three-hour unseen exams, usually papers from a previous year. The marks did not count towards our final results, but prepared us for writing under pressure and they were again marked by our tutors.

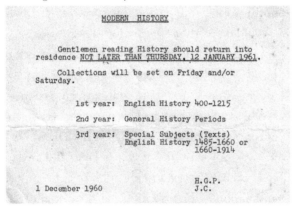

MODERN HISTORY

Gentlemen reading History should return into residence NOT LATER THAN THURSDAY, 12 JANUARY 1961.

Collections will be set on Friday and/or Saturday.

1st year:	English History 400-1215	
2nd year:	General History Periods	
3rd year:	Special Subjects (Texts) English History 1485-1660 or 1660-1914	

1 December 1960

H.G.P.
J.C.

Most of what we learnt came either from our tutor's comments, or from articles or books. We would read in the undergraduate library at the top of the spiral steps in Worcester, but it was not well equipped with recent books, though I found some strange Victorian on the dusty shelves. Most of our books, therefore, were in the Bodleian library, and particularly in the beautiful round Radcliffe Camera, where I spent much of my work time. I had very little money to buy books and depended almost entirely on libraries.

We also went to some lectures, though these were not compulsory and some people hardly went to any. Our tutors would recommend a few lecture series, but many felt that it was a waste of precious time breaking up a morning for a lecture. Finally there were seminars for two of the papers, the economic docu-ments and Cromwell special subject. Between six and a dozen students met their teacher for ninety minutes and one or two would read out longer papers and we would be expected to comment.

At the end of all of this intense teaching, a mixture of coaxing, scolding, praising, criticising, with largely self-motivated and self-organized work within a careful framework of supervised study, we would be ready, in theory, for the exams.

At the end of each term we would have to appear before the Provost (Head of College) and our tutors would report on our progress. They would also read out written reports from teachers in other Colleges if we had been studying elsewhere.

I had never been a high flyer, either at the Dragon or Sedbergh, and was not expected to get a First. But my tutor's letter after I received OFFICIAL notification of a Second shows that a combination of organization, hard work and genuine interest, had impressed some of the examiners.

Thus ended the final stage of my rite of transition from the infant born in the remote hills of Assam in the early years of the War, to an Oxford B.A., hopefully ready to put my first foot on the ladder of a successful career of some kind.

EIGHT

Metaphors for an Education

A USEFUL FRAMEWORK for understanding what happened to me is provided by the theory of the 'rite of passage' suggested by the French anthropologist Arnold van Gennep. Using his three-fold approach, which is a tool to understand when people are moved from one position (status) to another, the traumatic separation described in the preface fits in clearly as part of the first of the three phases of the 'rite of passage' or transition.

In Van Gennep's schema, the first stage is the separation off from the normal world, what he calls disaggregation. In this stage, an individual is taken out of his or her institutional setting and moved into a space which is outside the usual constraints and customs of the society. This space he terms liminality, the crossing of a threshold (*limen* in latin) into a parallel but marked off and separated world.

This first separating process is what the Dragon School to and other preparatory schools specialized in. They performed the extremely difficult task of taking us from our homes and families and settling us with complete strangers, both boys and adults. It was a painful process. Yet it was considered essential by our parents for it transferred us from the family to society. It moved us out of our birth group into a world where we were competitive individuals within an associational or contractual setting filled with non-relatives. The preparatory school was precisely the preparation for the next stage.

When we moved on to our public schools we entered an even more cut-off world, even more remote and liminal and not unlike the young people's puberty camps described by many anthropologists in Africa and elsewhere. There for five years we were subjected to the full force of elite English educational system. We started right at the bottom, as 'fags' or menial servants for older boys, and worked our way up to become prefects or minor rulers in our houses. We learnt how the English system of power, class and wealth worked through our progress up the various ladders of games, studies and classes. We internalized the mental, moral and social rules which underpin the kind of individualistic and capitalist system which we would have to operate in when we were adult. We learnt the rules of the game we were to play through our lives.

At the end of these five years of separation we were re-integrated into the world, but at a different level. Through going to Oxford, I was re-absorbed into wider upper middle class society. My history undergraduate degree and social life at Oxford would polish me and prepare me for whatever profession I entered after University. I began to return from my parallel world of boarding education into the fully adult world of wider English society. I was re-aggregated again, having moved through the process from childhood within a family to adulthood in a wider, non-family based, world.

* * *

ALAN MACFARLANE

While in one sense we went through a classic rite of passage, it is worth noting the ways in which my experience was the exact opposite of Van Gennep's schema. In Van Gennep's model, what changes is a person's status, roles and relationships. But not their mind, imagination, character or being. The process re-confirms and re-enforces the status quo. In the process, the normal inequalities of life are temporarily suspended in the liminal phase, and then after-re-aggregation they are re-asserted, but the individual has shifted, from pre-pubertal to pubertal, from unmarried to married, from alive to dead ancestor.

The English case parallels some of this structure - the dis-aggregation, liminality and re-aggregation. But what happens during this process is the exact opposite. In other words, in the public schools the emphasis is on inequality during the liminal stage (heavily marked differences in the status of junior and senior boys) and this is imposed as one of the central ways of learning about how future adult society works.

We were segregated, dis-aggregated, from the world in pre-paratory school and then deeply conditioned in what was in my day a harsh, physically challenging, highly controlled and restrictive forcing house at Public School. We were during term time deprived of personal space, privacy, food, quiet, leisure, girls, health and wealth. So that when these were all allowed back in as we re-emerged from isolation in our university years, we really appreciated them and looked at the world differently.

Almost all of life is about moving up ladders, from prepa-ratory school onwards. We were told that life is a struggle up various mountains, a race, a fight, a game we must win. In other words, the initial equality of being in a home and cherished as a member of a family who does not need to strive unduly to be loved, is turned into very strong hierarchical difference and then, after the liminal phase, we were re-absorbed as, separated, yet potentially equal person, through rite of transition culminating with our degree from university.

Just as games take two equal sides, place them in an arena and let them fight until one wins, and then shake hands and establish equality outside the arena, so the boarding education is an elaborate game, turning equality into temporary inequality, where you learn to 'play up, play up & play the game', and then at the end you re-emerge from the game, hopefully strengthened and better players, to play the game of life in the wider world.

* * *

My own education could well be seen as similar to growing a small fruit tree; the clipping and pruning, the manuring and weeding, an attempt to make me a 'fruitful' adult. Another metaphor can be taken from descriptions of the making of the Japanese samurai sword.

The first stage is to melt the ore and produce the raw iron for the finished project. My time in the womb, birth and infancy up to the time I returned to England aged five was this stage. This was when my body, mind and spirit were assembled and prepared for the later process. I was a set of raw metals waiting to be worked on, rough and fairly untamed.

Then the process starts which will be repeated numerous times. The iron is heated and made pliable, bent over and beaten to fuse it. It forms layers and while cooling it becomes stronger and stronger. This is the beating, shaping and strengthening which my 'preparatory' school started to do through physical and mental toughening. I ended up at the age of thirteen still small, but already quite tough and quite recognizable as the person I would be.

At my next school, a single-sex boarding school, this was repeated more severely. As my body and mind grew more rapidly, I was constantly hammered both physically and mentally. So by sixteen I was already a pretty tough late adolescent.

Now the sharpening and further beating began and in my last two years at this school my teachers tried to give a sufficient 'edge', an ability to cut through and understand ideas at a level which would get me into a good university. By the time I arrived at Oxford as an undergraduate I was a rather rough but serviceable sword.

The undergraduate years were dedicated to polishing the blade so that by the time I finished I would be ready for any professional task or training - administrative, educational, legal, medical, business or religious.

The professional path I then chose at the age of twenty-one was academic and intellectual, to train to be a university teacher. This meant further refining and sharpening, especially of the creative point of the sword. If I was to discover new ideas and discredit old ones, to provide a model and an education for my future pupils, I had to know how to do research. I needed to know how to master materials and then to communicate my new knowledge through books and articles.

So the final sharpening of the sword took place and by the end of my doctorate, when I was twenty-four, I was, in principle, ready for my career as an academic. I was also socially, economically and politically ready for the next stage in my life, namely to marry and to reproduce myself through my children.

The process I am describing for myself is a double one. On the one hand I needed to be separated off, made into a single atom, detached from too strong attachments to people or institutions. I had to be turned from being a member of a birth-given 'community' to becoming a member of free-floating and amorphous 'society'.

I needed to be 'free' to transact in the market economy in the sense that Adam Smith or Karl Marx described; a free believer in my own ideology and religion in the way Max Weber suggested; a contractual and autonomous political animal in the way in which Hobbes and Locke had described.

To change the metaphor, I had to be cut loose from all moorings and the little craft that I was becoming had to be set free to bob off into the ocean of society. Continuing this nautical metaphor, I needed to be made sturdy, more or less unsinkable by even the largest gale.

So my preparatory school was a period when the shape of the boat was determined, even if it was rather miniature, and the main framework was put in place. My public school was when the boat was made larger and the planks were securely nailed in place. It was now nearly sea-worthy. Oxford was when the tar and protective paint was applied and decking put on to prevent the waves flooding the boat.

By the end of these three stages, I had turned from the wobbly raft, an assembly of bits of wood and petrol cans held together by rope which had arrived back in England at the age of five, to the sturdy, if not hugely elegant ocean-going vessel that finished up after six years at Oxford.

To further expand the metaphor, I was both the boat and also the navigator. My outer shell of body and character was to keep me afloat, but what I would do on my life's voyage, how I would navigate and how deal with the rocks, tides and pirates, would be the result of the navigational tools and sailing skills which I learnt through the process.

The history, geography, English, maths, language, religion, and above all the cast of mind, which included humour and an ability to see myself as others saw me, were the tools for the voyage. These were the skills, maps and supplies, which would either ensure my survival or lead me to disaster.

Now all these metaphors of an English education strike me as rather prosaic. Surely, it might be thought by many contemporary British or Americans, this is the obvious way in which to turn an infant into an efficient and operating member of a modern society? Yet a brief acquaintance with how education works in other contexts shows that what I underwent was comparatively rather unusual.

Simplifying greatly, in other cases the goal is very different. The aim is not to hammer out a sword, or to make a sturdy boat with a crew of one, or perhaps two at the most (in companionate marriage). The aim elsewhere is not to separate off the individual from the group, but rather to make him or her a more effective member of the group. Most societies are not based on contract, but on birth-given status, they are relational (people are not separable atoms), people are not to be trained to be actors who alone encompass the four spheres of life.

* * *

In some ways, the stages of education could be seen as a parallel to the four stages of human history. My infancy in India was hunter-gatherer, living in a world of immediate return, small family groups, mobile, without many formal institutional structures that I was aware of. There was very little remembered history, formal religion or complex material culture. Simplicity and flexibility were the dominant virtues, especially in the war years of 1941-5.

The Dragon period was one of tribalism – of oral, group-based, holistic, ritualistic, embedded life – with again little hierarchy, little wider institutional structure, a great deal of the custom which guides tribes. These were the Dragon and Dorset Days.

Then came the State, formal Religion, an instituted economy, villages (houses) and a settled hierarchy – with rulers and ruled and increasing discipline. These were Sedbergh Days, a peasant civilization, where writing was increasingly important and institutional structures more visible.

The University took the peasant and turned him into a modern person – with the formal separations, the heightened stress on science and rationality, questioning, conflict, relativism, suspended judgements, the grey world of adulthood. Yet this was all built on the previous, still present, layers, from hunter-gatherer onwards.

So the adult who was formed was a composite of all the stages rolled into one – and I have had to travel backwards to the start to see them all. This is one reason why all the periods of education have to be integrated and written together in order to see the total development and the interconnectivity of the patterns that join together the past.

The schools and university were taking us out of the 'pre-modern' world of our infancy and childhood, into the adult world which managed to preserve two systems alongside each other, a modern scientific material, rational and logical world, with hints of a non-scientific, artistic, integrated, familistic, magical, parallel world. The same mixture occurred with social structure and leisure, which was both individualistic, exploitative and capitalistic, but mixed with irrational elements of trust, friendship, anti-capitalist/individualistic mentality and morality.

ALAN MACFARLANE

How We
Understand the World

THIS BOOK IS part of a series of short letters written to young friends. Encouraged by the reception of my *Letters to Lily* (2005), I decided to write a set of letters to her younger sister – Reflections for Rosa. I was then asked by other friends to write short books for their children.

In each I try to explore some aspect of 'How We Understand the World,' based on my experience as an anthropologist and historian at Cambridge University. I have tried to put into simple words what I have learnt about discovery, creativity and methods to understand our complex world.

CAM RIVERS
PUBLISHING

Image on front cover is an adaptation of Temperance (Temperantia) from The
Virtues by Pieter Bruegel the Elder, available in the public domain.

Made in the USA
Columbia, SC
26 July 2018